Born in Melbourne, **Jeff O'Hare** has been an Anglican priest for 21 years. He is the chaplain to the Brotherhood of St Laurence and vicar of St Philip's Church, Collingwood, as well as having a pastoral connection to the Choir of Hard Knocks. Prior to this he was senior chaplain to Geelong Grammar School and its rural campus Timbertop. Jeff has had a lifelong interest in social justice and was a theological student attached to the Brotherhood in 1987. He has known many Brotherhood clients over the years and has developed strong ongoing relationships with many of those that the organisation cares for.

Peter McConchie worked for more than ten years internationally as a professional photographer. Since his return to Australia he has had a number of photography books published, including *Yolngu Mali: Aboriginal Spirit*, *Old Growth: Australia's Remaining Ancient Forests*, *Point Nepean* and *Elders: Wisdom from Australia's Indigenous Leaders*. He is passionate about environmental and indigenous issues and believes strongly in reconciliation and inclusion.

Brotherhood
of St Laurence

Working for an Australia free of poverty

Brotherhood

Stories of Courage and Resilience

Fr Jeff O'Hare

Photography by Peter McConchie

to Sammy Langevin's school that we might always be kind and good listeners to those in need.

VIKING

an imprint of

PENGUIN BOOKS

VIKING

Published by the Penguin Group
Penguin Group (Australia)
250 Camberwell Road, Camberwell, Victoria 3124, Australia
(a division of Pearson Australia Group Pty Ltd)

New York   Toronto   London   Dublin   New Delhi
Auckland   Johannesburg

Penguin Books Ltd, Registered Offices: 80 Strand, London, WC2R 0RL, England

First published by Penguin Group (Australia), 2009

10 9 8 7 6 5 4 3 2 1

The moral right of the author and photographer have been asserted

These stories capture only an instant in the lives of the individuals interviewed, and
it is important to remember that beliefs, relationships and memories all change over
time. The information here is correct at time of writing.

Cover and text design by Marley Flory © Penguin Group (Australia), 2009
Photography by Peter McConchie
Typeset in 10.5/19 pt Else NPL by Post Pre-press Group, Brisbane, Queensland
Scanning by Splitting Image P/L, Clayton, Victoria
Printed in Australia by McPhersons Printing Group, Maryborough, Victoria

Cataloguing information for this book is available from the
National Library of Australia

ISBN 9780670071951

penguin.com.au

Contents

Foreword by Russell Crowe

It doesn't take much for life to alter course, and for our well-made plans to dramatically change. A sudden illness, the loss of a job, or a shift in family dynamics, can create crisis and challenge for any one of us.

The courageous people who have opened up their lives to us in this book are still dealing with the consequences of adversity. Their stories, as well as being honest and compelling, are vibrant with love, friendship and a sense of community.

My life is about telling stories through film and I appreciate the extraordinary in the ordinary. Stories open our hearts to worlds beyond our own and invite deeper understanding. Where there is understanding our love expands.

Many of us live, more or less, on one side of advantage. It is a great gift from each of those who have told their stories in these pages to share with us their joys and sorrows, their faith and doubts. Their resilience and their generosity are a lesson to us all. God bless them.

Thank you to those who have prepared this book and given support through the Brotherhood of St Laurence.

Acknowledgements

Nothing could have prepared me for the emotional roller-coaster that writing this book took me on. It was a journey, yes, but also a privilege because these stories are so moving, real and raw. Often, when sitting at the feet of someone who is dying, I have heard great reflections, sometimes confessional, on a life lived and on the anticipation of its end. But in these stories, life is in full swing. I am proud to be part of an organisation where the depth of understanding, the transformation, and the freedoms won have made all the difference to those that we care for.

Reconciliation comes through relationships and the opening of doors. No matter what our perceived capacities, there is always a possibility that through meeting the right person or carer we might be challenged to think of another way to live, or to simply accept the help that will begin to put us back on track. What so many of us take for granted, these remarkable people have not had. However, they have each tasted a freedom through the extraordinary relationships they have developed with workers, communities and neighbourhoods. This connection has allowed them the space to live a life that is worthy of their capacity to engage. Each one has generously given back to the community in which they find themselves. These are wonderful, real stories, and these people are our friends.

My thanks to each of you for trusting me to tell your story. This is your book, and you also represent thousands whose stories are yet to be told and honoured.

I would like to thank Lyn Amy for her work in developing this project, and our publisher, Penguin Books, for their belief in the book. My particular thanks to Jo Turner, and to Sarah Dawson for her wonderful editorial support.

My gratitude also to some people who have helped me to complete *Brotherhood*. Helene Durkin, who patiently typed as I spoke, and sweated with me over the beginning of each story. Michelle Low, my collaborator, who kept me on track and offered such positive feedback.

Thanks to Peter McConchie for his sensitive and beautiful portraits. Tony Nicholson, the Executive Director of the Brotherhood, for his encouragement, and his clear mind on the nature of the human spirit which has made sense of all this. Tom and Margo Hartley for their continued support of my endeavours and their real support of this book.

Thanks also to Debra Saffrey Collins, who mentors and knows me well enough to be a constructive critic. And to Craig Miller, for his generous incentive to complete what was started, for helping me understand why the presence of a good friend makes all the difference.

Father Jeff O'Hare

Chaplain and Executive Team Member,

Brotherhood of St Laurence

Photographer's Note

It has certainly been a humbling experience to be the photographer for *Brotherhood* and to have the opportunity to work with the wonderful people in its pages. In many ways, the Brotherhood of St Laurence operates as a community and extended family, whose members (previously known as 'clients') look out for one another. Within the world of the Brotherhood there are no social prejudices; people from all walks of life are represented here. Much can be learned at the Brotherhood, and from the unexpected teachers within this book.

Peter McConchie

petermcconchie@iprimus.com.au

Introduction

A strong commitment and determination to end social injustice is central to every aspect of the work undertaken by the Brotherhood of St Laurence. We are dedicated to working for an Australia free of poverty.

Father Tucker, who founded the Brotherhood of St Laurence 78 years ago, understood that every person, no matter what their station, wishes to be part of the mainstream economic and social life of our community. Since then, time and time again, the Brotherhood's daily work has demonstrated that deep down even the poorest of the poor hold modest mainstream aspirations: to be able to work; to have a decent home; to experience family; and to be part of the wider community. Unfortunately, in recent decades, this image of disadvantaged Australians has been all but lost. As a result, much of the public policy designed to tackle poverty has inevitably fallen short of its objectives.

The Brotherhood is committed to understanding the lived experience of disadvantaged people, in order that policy and services can be shaped in the most effective way. That is why, from its very beginnings, the Brotherhood has devoted great effort to hearing the voices of disadvantaged Australians through careful listening and through high quality social research. This way we can ensure that the services we offer and our social policy prescriptions are grounded in accurate images of them.

In the Great Depression of the 1930s, Father Tucker used film to enable people to tell their stories. Today, in this book, we have a collection of stories about people we help, written by Father Jeff O'Hare, the Brotherhood Chaplain. Jeff is in the unique and privileged position of fostering the spiritual dimension of the large, sprawling and complex community that is the modern Brotherhood. The role of the chaplain is special, and his relationship with each of the people who have sat and shared their stories for this book is unconditional. Through their experiences, we begin to understand the reality of what life can be like for many people in our community.

Jeff has a unique gift for identifying the strengths and courage of the people he meets in his work here at the Brotherhood. So often we mistakenly see others as victims, while the truth is that we are all fellow citizens in need of help, support and companionship, and with our own valuable contribution to make. That is the universal experience.

So often we categorise people as 'other', we think of them as somehow different, we push them to the margins and imagine that they are not like us. If you read these stories carefully you will recognise that each of the individuals who has been courageous and generous enough to share their life with us is a person just like you and me.

Through their memories of family, loss, tragedy and triumph we see that every human life is precious, regardless of social standing, wealth or power. We see that a little of a higher being dwells within all of us. And we are challenged to allow that bit of the higher being in each of us to meet that bit of the higher being that dwells steadfastly within our disadvantaged neighbour. These stories encourage us to walk in the shoes of our fellow man – and to walk humbly with our God.

Tony Nicholson

Executive Director, Brotherhood of St Laurence

David Nyuol
Vincent

Where do courage and bravery start? Is it contextual? Does what a young person sees and experiences form them and their actions for the rest of their life?

David Vincent is an inspiration; his story is inspirational. It is harrowing, and the events he has witnessed we would do everything in our power to protect our children from. He has seen more than most of us would ever want to see in a whole lifetime.

Born in the Sudan in the mid-1980s, in a little town called Wau, David was three when war broke out there. David's father, a lawyer, an educated man, became the target of the northern government's Islamic sector, which planned to eradicate such people as a means of making the 'Christian south' powerless. A friend of the family informed David's father that he was on the 'hit list' and that he should get out of the district as soon as he could. David's mother was pregnant and not in a position to travel, so she was left behind. With his father, David began a perilous six-week journey, surviving on wild food – fruit, the leaves of trees, and wild animals. David was lucky because he was with his dad, so he was protected, unlike some children who were on their own and had no one to look out for them; many were taken by lions. David remembers the agony of the long walk and, like any child, constantly asking his father, 'When are we reaching Ethiopia?' His father would reply, 'Tomorrow, tomorrow.'

'People were lying on the footpaths, dead. Dad would reassure me they were only sleeping.'

When they finally arrived in Ethiopia, they were met by the UN Refugee Agency (UNHCR), which had requisitioned a site for a refugee camp. It was a big space in the middle of a forest, with no facilities or resources. They started building temporary shelters, but still had no food or running water: they survived on leaves, and used a nearby river for drinking and washing. 'After a month, we began to receive medical attention and food.' As the threat against him lifted, David's dad was 'retrained' and sent home for work. David, just four, was left behind to look after himself.

'There was an outbreak of cholera and many people died; we had to bury our own friends. I became very ill with diarrhoea and was put in hospital, isolated in a tent with other sick children. There was little medicine, so you just rode it out. After three or four days, I was strong enough to go outside and breathe some air. When I returned the others were gone. They had died, and I was sent back to rejoin the main group.'

David was in this refugee camp for four years, with few amenities and little support. 'There was no proper school or teachers, so we started to draw on the floor and to teach ourselves.'

In May 1991, war broke out again in Ethiopia and the refugees were forced back into the Sudan. The Sudanese were not keen on refugees, particularly their own, and as many crossed the border, swimming across the Gilo river, they were shot. David and his cohort ran along the river away from enemy fire, until they could cross the river safely.

Once in the Sudan, David says, the threat to his life increased. 'The government sent bombers to bomb the refugees on a daily basis. We dug holes and tunnels, and lived underground from sunrise to sunset every day so they couldn't see us. The holes were deep enough that if they did bomb us, we were safe. After dark, we would come out to look for food, which was scarce. For eight months, things got worse.

'So began the walk to Kenya. A month's walk. We finally arrived at the border, at a town called Lokichogio, and spent a year there. It was safe, a different zone, and the northern government couldn't touch us there. But the camp was the same as the last camp, and we had to start again.

'We were taken by Red Cross trucks to Kakuma refugee camp. It was the same routine: we were given small tents and sheets of plastic and building materials; there was little food, not enough for everybody, so we broke up into groups and combined the supplies. Some groups had ten to twelve people; ours was 50. The food would last two weeks if we only had one meal per day, just dinner. Once again there were no schools and we started one under the trees. It was our own. We got exercise books which we cut in half so two people would benefit from one.'

'There were no schools and we started one under the trees. It was our own.'

Later a settlement program started for the children, and many were sent to the USA. David's time did not come and he was left alone when his friends were sent, left to cry for those he had travelled with for so long.

David remained in the camp for the next thirteen years; he continued to study, finished high school and learnt English. With still no contact from his family, he decided to go back to the Sudan to try to find them. He sent an email to a friend who had found a passage to Australia. His friend urged him to apply to come here and sent David the application forms. The process took two years and David finally arrived in Australia in 2004; he had just turned 22.

In Melbourne, David faced a whole lot of new challenges. 'Here is a totally different way of life. I came with no expectations of anything at all – my focus was on getting out of the context in which the whole of my life had happened. It was all new and I literally had to start again!' He arrived in the middle of a cold winter, nothing like he had ever experienced; a country even with a different climate. 'I got mixed up when I first arrived and kept thinking to myself, what do I have to do to make it all work?'

He gained a place at Melbourne University with the help of a social worker, though given what he had come through he was not confident about getting in. The assessment was based on his English skills, which he had been diligent in developing while in the refugee camp in Kenya. He took sciences – chemistry, biology and physics – and passed them all. He was granted a scholarship, which has helped him greatly. He has also begun a degree in criminology, about which he is passionate, and would like to pursue a career in 'Intelligence'. He did particularly well with his studies in 2005 and is contemplating studying community development.

David started to search for his parents and, surprisingly, found them very quickly. They had never got back together: his father had assumed his mother had been killed, and had remarried; they live in different villages. In 2007, David made the trip back to the Sudan to meet them. His mother couldn't believe he was still alive, and in fact refused to go to the airport because she didn't think it could be him.

On his return to Australia, David deferred his degree and went to work to raise money to help his family. 'I need to raise 500 dollars a month to help my parents and my brother. They don't enjoy good health and the support is vital to keep them well. Sometimes it costs more than that. I wire the money through a bank here and it arrives in the Sudan at the villages where my family live. A businessman brokers the money from that end, and you have to trust that it is happening, which means a lot of goodwill. Supporting them has to be my priority at the moment.' He hopes to take up study part-time in the next year to complete what he has started.

David is now a youth ambassador with the Victorian Human Rights Commission. His role is to talk to schools and church community groups about his journey, and about human rights and the plight of many of his country's people. He came in contact with the Brotherhood of St Laurence by becoming a volunteer with our Breakfast Club at Atherton Gardens in Fitzroy, supporting our refugee children with breakfast and conversational support on their way to school each morning. He now works with our Napier Street children's programs as a support to families still suffering the effects of their long journey to freedom and their settlement in

Melbourne; he also works at the Centre for Multicultural Youth, based in Carlton. He has been motivated enough to seek out these places for himself, and his experience and passion to help those who have suffered the same traumas he did are impressive and inspirational. Everybody who meets him feels the potential and special qualities that are manifest in his work, in his concern and advocacy. We at the Brotherhood would be worse off for not having run with this gift that landed amongst us, full of hope and gratitude, and an urgency to transform the lives of others. Thank you for finding us, David.

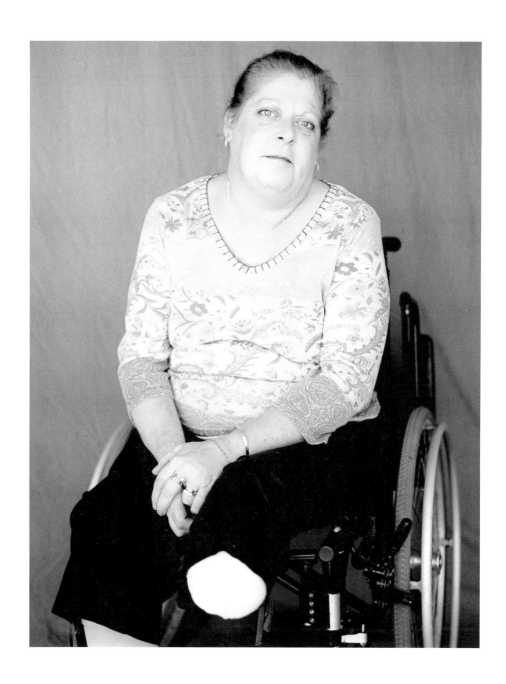

Debra Thomas

Like many suburbs along the railway line between Melbourne and the bayside city of Frankston, Edithvale is subject to heavy traffic and the regular clanging of level-crossing bells. There is a certain sparseness because of the lack of trees, and the area is dominated by wires, boom gates and shopping strips.

As I step into Debra Thomas's world, a newish small unit opposite a railway crossing, it is like stepping into somebody's soul. Her home is full of colour: as she says herself, 'God dropped a huge box of colour into our world, many mediums of creativity and life'. Debra is an artist and she uses these media to express her great gift; her art really does come from the heart.

We move through her front room, its walls covered in paintings and more leaning against them, an easel in the middle of the room. In the kitchen and family room there are boxes of crayons and coloured pencils, sketchbooks and journals, along with completed art and craft works, and for a moment you feel overwhelmed that this could be the many facets of one person. Debra can see that I'm impressed and the conversation begins quickly and easily; we like each other and she is comfortable with both abstract discussion and her own raw story.

She admits that at times she finds it difficult to trust people. I empathise with her feelings because I see that she's physically vulnerable. She has spent a lot of time in hospital, having had one leg amputated in 2001 and the other in 2006. Debra attends the City Life Jubilee Christian Church and she has asked for the prayers of its pastor; she believes in the power of healing and she wants to be able to walk independently. She also has other physical and medical conditions owing to a mixture of drug addiction and alcoholism, which resulted from depression and breakdown over her life's journey. For a lot of her time she's fairly housebound.

She talks of her parents: 'Mum was raised out in the country and lost her father at the age of eleven. Her brother Gary used to be a sheep shearer. Because of the tough life my mother lived, she tells me that her brother used to make her rabbit-skin shoes, after he had skinned the bunny and eaten the meat! I believe in my heart of hearts Mum did the very best she could with me, and I believe that both my parents loved me equally as much. Dad, who died some time ago, was a full-on drill sergeant who served in the Middle East during the Second World War and was a prisoner of war. He had a horrendous life and was a hard man to please. He passed all that hardness on to his children and would often comment that he had

had a really tough life, so we would too.' Debra comments here, 'I'd really like to say that despite everything negative that happened, there was ten-fold more of love and family life for me and my brothers and sisters. I don't believe that my pain is worse than anyone else's. On the scale it all weighs up equal.'

> The colours she uses represent Jesus and protection; through art she rejoices both in her freedom to express herself and in her faith.

Debra has found God 'for real' and she points out that she has most of the Scripture on her MP3 player; in the background there are Christian songs playing. She tells us that the colours she uses represent Jesus and protection, and that through art she rejoices both in her freedom to express herself and in her faith. She tells us she has an altar because she can't get to church as much as she would like, that at this altar she can be with Jesus, shut the door and talk and pray.

'My daughter Sarah is 24 years old and normally lives in the area, but at the moment she's at Lismore Heights College in New South Wales where she is studying hard. Her ambition is to take up a medical degree. I'm so proud of her because of her determination and because we have such a great relationship – although we still have our moments – and our friendship still shines in my heart.' Debra shows me some of their correspondence; Sarah's letters and photos all come with an assurance that she loves her mum, that's she exploring her own faith. Her letters end with 'God's blessing and love'.

Debra's second child, Michael, is 21 and she's uncomfortable with the fact that he is interested in Buddhism. She says she warns him that at the end he will have to face his own stuff on his own before God.

Deb was born in New South Wales in 1963 and the family moved to Mornington in southern Victoria when she was two. 'Dad was still with the army. I was number five of six children and life was pretty hard. We learnt what to do by what we couldn't or shouldn't do – punishment reigned supreme with both Mum and Dad; though, we were told, nothing that happened to us ever compared to what they had been through, so we couldn't complain. It was so tough that I became restless and at the age of fourteen I just stopped going to school. I got a job splitting scallops in a factory and used to wear plastic over my shoes and stand for hours on a concrete floor. Later I got a job sewing at a factory and I just couldn't go back to school.

'Because I was the fifth child, Mum and Dad never bothered taking photos of me and there were virtually none of me before I was four. How much would it have taken to get the camera out and take a photo?' Debra would just lie on the sofa and watch *Days of Our Lives*. She didn't feel safe at school because things were violent there; when she looks back now, she can't believe this was her life.

Debra found that to survive she had to reinvent herself many times over. She has been creative all her life; she kept visual diaries and produced drawings and abstract images from a very early age. It was her way of coping with the harsh realities of her childhood.

She went to live in a caravan in Carrum at the age of fifteen, with no social benefits. It was hard to get to work, so she moved to Frankston and lived with some bikies. For a short time she had a job with a Japanese company making wiring looms for cars. It was tough trying to make it in the work force at this young age.

Sarah was born before Debra married; then she had Michael. At around this time her brother hanged himself and she was full of hurt in her heart over him doing it.

'I trashed myself after that and started taking whatever drugs I could find – and more. I discovered I could not cope and I didn't want to feel anything. I am part of a big family, but we weren't close and I just did not feel that I could go to them for help. My husband – I'm still married – lives in Mornington. He's a good father but a bastard of a husband; but you only get married once, so the Bible says.'

She is generous and her space exudes a sense of abundance. She maintains she's an honest person, which is important to her and wrapped up in her relationship with Jesus, who, she reckons, can change 'shit to sugar because he has changed me!' We laugh at that; it's quite an image.

As Debra said, everything caught up with her in later life and she had a complete emotional breakdown, which in turn caused a physical breakdown. She stopped eating and drinking, and just drank alcohol and used drugs. One day she went to hospital because she had a sore leg and the doctors discovered that her whole body was shutting down. Now her legs are gone, her kidneys don't work well and she lives with an ileostomy bag; there are times still when she herself just has to shut down emotionally.

Debra was discovered one day by Lisa Astete, a community contact officer with the Brotherhood, while she was living (or, as she says, 'stuck') at the supportive residential unit in Frankston. Debra felt like a prisoner there and had even contemplated suicide; it was difficult to see her children, who were at the time struggling with what had happened to their mother. Through Lisa and others at the Brotherhood, Debra was able to find housing and to connect with an art group at Cube 37, the creative-arts space at Frankston Arts Centre. This group gives her life and a place to express

Every day is a fight for life; everything is problematic and must be negotiated.

her extraordinary creativity. While she sees Jesus as her connecting spirit in all these things, her daughter Sarah gives her life as well. It hasn't been easy, but despite the roller-coaster of her life she remains hopeful and supported for the journey ahead.

Every day is a fight for life; everything is problematic and must be negotiated.

Sometimes, says Debra, she feels utterly alone and tired and sick of everything. But there are lights in her world: her children, her home help, the art classes and her wonderful physiotherapist. 'And there is Jesus, who carries me, who makes me thankful.'

I feel a real tug at our parting, I kiss her on the cheek and promise to come back for a cup of tea very soon.

Simon Mansell

Simon's fame and popularity have risen through his member-ship of the Choir of Hard Knocks. He has won the hearts of many for his gentle, self-effacing nature, and his ever-changing hair colours and styles. Then there's his layered clothing, always adorned with his heavy warm overcoat – no matter what the weather – and his many rings and bracelets, all of which hold significance in his relationship to the 'powers beyond' and his interaction with them.

I arrive to collect Simon. He has recently reconnected with his father and they decided it would be good to spend Christmas together at his father's home in Alice Springs. This was a signifi-cant step in Simon's life, and no doubt his father's too, and there is an air of almost childish excitement as I pick Simon up at 6 a.m. to drive him to Melbourne Airport to make the journey north.

The plane doesn't leave until 9 a.m., but he is anxious and doesn't want to miss the flight. We park the car, drag his very heavy suitcase to the terminal, and I show him how to book in on one of the computer desks that stand like sentinels in all the wrong places. The people at the check-in counter are polite; in fact, they can't stop smiling and nodding knowingly and encouragingly at Simon in his big coat, despite his suitcase weighing in at 37 kilos!

We get to the security check-in and Simon sails through, along with untold bangles, buckles and rings, without any problems. I follow, and alarms go off all over the place; before we know it, I am removing my shoes and belt and am being asked to receive a drug scan. As Simon looks on, a little bemused that it's me and not him, he finally laughs out loud in front of the equally bemused security man, who has noticed my priest's collar. 'Just as well it's you and not me, eh, Father Jeff!' The little man looks embarrassed, and as he finds nothing that would throw me into jail, I put my shoes and belt back on, retaining what little dignity I have left as hundreds of people stream past looking at the priest 'getting busted'!

I buy Simon breakfast – a Hungry Jack's burger and a large Coke – and he finds a smoking platform, to which he returns several times over the next hour. As we walk towards the gate lounge, he insists very politely that I buy him a present to mark the occasion. Simon is a lovable character, and I feel compelled to oblige: another ring and a 'snow dome' of Melbourne are finally selected. Later, we sit in the lounge and talk about what it might be like to spend some time with his dad. There is a beauty, an innocence, in his excitement, and it is wonderfully moving to have the privilege of being with him at that moment. Then he is away, and 95 dollars later I am driving back towards the Brotherhood office, happy for the adventure.

Simon Paul Mansell was born in the Princess Margaret Hospital in Perth, Western Australia, on 29 June 1976, to Karen Hanson and Brent Mansell. He grew up in Perth, but for much of his early life the family was unsettled and moved frequently, often to escape from conflict – to Fremantle, North Fremantle, Bribrilay, Denmark, Swanbourne and Mt Helen – sometimes in a caravan, sometimes with grandparents. Simon had three brothers: Ezra, who died soon after birth; Luke, who was born in 1978; and Stephen, born in 1981.

Once, the whole family were in the car and Simon remembers this occasion well because he was frightened. There was a fight over putting Stephen in the 'baby seat', and he ended up on his mother's knee in the front; there were empty beer bottles in the car. Simon was scared and he had hidden on the floor behind the driver's seat; Luke was in the back seat. The car ran off the road and hit a light pole at high speed. Mother and baby Stephen were killed instantly; Dad had a shattered jaw; and the beer bottles seemed to explode, leaving Luke deeply lacerated by fragments of glass.

'For years broken glass oozed out of Luke's skin. I was knocked unconscious, but I remember clearly my fear and how, before I woke, I had a vision in which my mum stood before me and said goodbye, holding baby Stephen in her arms. I just knew that something terrible was going to happen on that journey, and it was as though I just made myself ready for the worst. I just knew, Father Jeff, I know things like that.'

After years of turmoil and trouble, violence and unhappiness, as the family struggled to stay afloat after the death of his mother and brother, Simon ran away from home. 'I met a girl and camped out with a mate. I separated myself from my family and quit my job. I tried acid for the first time. After five or six trips, I freaked out and ended up in hospital; that's when my mental health problems really started.' In the midst of poverty and upheaval, Simon discovered a gift for poetry. He had found what he loved to do, and what he was good at. Realistic enough to see that his writing could not sustain him, he had to do what he describes as 'menial jobs' to sustain himself in the pursuit of his passion. 'Poetry is what I really love and I worked as hard at this as anyone would working at anything else.'

Eventually Simon left Western Australia, and he arrived in Sydney during the bushfires of 2000–2001. He slept on the streets and later showed me the hidey-holes and garden beds in and around Hyde Park that he had found for himself. He commented how sleeping rough wasn't so bad in Sydney, because it was warmer than Melbourne. In 2007, back in Sydney to make his debut at the Sydney Opera House with the Choir of Hard Knocks, he laughed as he reflected on the fact that only a few years before he had been sleeping on these very streets.

Simon eventually found his way to Melbourne. There, at his nightly haunt, the Fitzroy soup kitchen, he was found by two 'angels' called Michael and Jenny, who were looking for volunteers to join a street choir. What evolved from that night was the unfolding of his dream, his passion, and the moment when finally he felt appreciated 'for the gift of himself'. The Choir of Hard Knocks has become the place where Simon, in the midst of this large city, feels honoured, appreciated, understood, accepted. He has the opportunity to express himself through singing, and has at times found the right and the courage to express his opinions, especially on what he sees as injustices; hope is back in his step.

One day Simon asked me for baptism into the Christian faith. We would sit outside week after week (because he needs to smoke and to drink gallons of coffee) and talk about God and about spirits – his connection with things that lie beyond. He understands the concepts, the Jesus story, the example, and the potential of life in all its fullness. He likens it to his own 'spiritual' experiences. Simon of Cyrene helped Jesus carry his cross to the Crucifixion, so he has a connection to that story too.

The day I baptised him at St Philip's, it was just me and him and a few others. He had arrived that day, tapped me on the shoulder and said, 'Today's the day, Father Jeff.' He had chosen a sponsor to stand with him, but as we began our Church's most important sacramental rite, members of the Choir of Hard Knocks came in one by one to watch. By the time we poured water over his head and spoke the sacred words, the church was full.

As Simon lifted his head to receive the sign of the Cross on his forehead, and a lit candle was placed in his hand, the crowd cheered and cried and thumped him on the back, and Simon said to me, 'You see, Father Jeff, I told you they'd come'. Afterwards, as the choir had their evening meal before going on their way, Simon came to me and said; 'When you made the sign of the Cross, there was heat in it and I can still feel it.'

Simon sings a part in what has become the choir's signature song, 'Hallelujah'. He, like each of the soloists as they sing, brings the song to life. It is as though the words are part of them. As Simon sings, the words become his story, and the depth and agony of his journey gives him a chance to tell his audience, who have grown to love him, something of himself. It is for all of us, choir members and listeners, a humbling moment. He is Simon, he helped.

Simon laughs, and his world is full of colours, his rings and wrist bracelets all signs of the spiritual world and symbols of his journey – of his deep feelings, of the love and the hate that have been present in his life from time to time. He still sees visions, like the one he saw of his mother and little brother on the day they were killed. There are also voices at times, but there are dreams too. He feels that he has a gift of special power, of magic, but he is quick to add that 'with power comes great responsibility and wouldn't it be a sad world if there was no magic'. In his worst moments he is visited by demons, but in his newfound gift he envisages the ascent of his life into God's.

I sit here looking out
Peering from the valley below,
Looking for all the restless faces
With nowhere to go.
Their eyes have faded, their minds set
To chase the grind of day
As I sit here without a clock
Searching for another today.

Hearts of steel
The eyes of men are blind
Hearts of steel
The eyes of the world committed suicidal blindness.

The highway pulls its belt
Sweat wiped away from chins
All the wrinkled suits and ties
Can feel a hanging from within

Faces all turned purple all hands numb
Driving behind their wheels of fate
With some small child scream'n out
Let the cool air in.
A train pulls into shore
I'm waiting by the side of the way

All things I once stood for
Has turned all faces away
There must be more, I can't be sure
For tomorrow to shape today
As my hands all blistered and bruised
Turn to face the dawn of day.

Simon Mansell

Pat Parker

I've known Pat for about a year, and have got to know her well through both my visits to the Coolibah Centre, the Brotherhood's drop-in centre, and the Choir of Hard Knocks. Pat has always encouraged my work and given me great feedback. It was Pat who originally took me down to meet the choir and it has been thanks to her that they now have a rehearsal space at St Philip's, where I am the minister.

I was keen to tell Pat's story. She is a woman who has found a level of peace in life through offering her experience and her care to other people. Everything she does is in consideration of others and every day her main focus is on how she can help someone else. Recently one of her distant relatives died, leaving her with a small inheritance. She gave most of the money to her brother so that he could set himself up with a home; she also gave the parish a donation so that we could help those in need in our area. The rest she spent on a new dress for her performances with the choir. Now in her late 60s she is an example of social justice at work in daily life.

The Second World War was all but over when Pat Parker was born, on 8 June 1943 at the Royal Women's Hospital in Melbourne. She remembers from her childhood the lingering whispers, the coupons for food and clothing, the making-do. 'We were happy, yet we had nothing new, only second-hand things.' What was significant for Pat was happiness: parents who were happy together, and hard-working too, a happiness that 'came through to us and on us'; a childhood of simple fun they made for themselves. She recalls the streets of her suburb, Richmond, filled with children playing and mothers standing on their front doorsteps, while dads and husbands were at work.

'Growing up in Melbourne was great. Richmond was very working-class; all the men worked and the women stayed at home with the kids. The streets were full of kids and you made your own fun . . . real family life. If you didn't know a kid on the street, you made sure you got to know them!'

Pat's dad, Alfred, was a manager of the Mountain View Hotel in Bridge Road, Richmond. He was a hard worker and trusted employee, whose generous boss gave him 200 pounds as a deposit towards the family's new home in Clayton. Pat's mum, Gladys, stayed at home and looked after Pat and her brothers Robert and Bruce.

Pat attended St Ignatius Catholic School in Richmond in her early years. Her first paid job was in a paper shop; later she worked for a bookbinder and then in a dress shop. She was happy earning eight shillings a week. She met Thomas at the pictures when she was sixteen, and they married on 17 March 1961 at the Registry Office. 'It was easier, quicker and cheaper than the church, to do it this way.' They lived in Noble Park, Dandenong and Doveton, and had five children: Darren, Michael, Christine, Nicole and Lori.

'The early years were great, and life went on.' But in time the marriage became violent, and despite the advice of a Catholic priest to 'stick with it', Pat moved to Fitzroy to live with friends. 'This was a tough time, and I relied on the generosity of many people. Towards the end with Thomas, it was terrible: things would be fine for the first few days of the week, but then on Thursday – pay day – he'd get on the booze and would become violent. If you were in his way when he came towards you, look out! I used all the excuses in the world for the bruises. It was a real shock, I'd never known anything like this. I'd had such a happy life up until then.

'After it was over, I stopped being just a social drinker. I had a beer at a party when I was 30, and it just took over. People would say I looked good and I drank to celebrate that – to please others. I became an alcoholic and ended up at AA meetings. That blew me away, as there was a room full of people – professionals, well-known people, actors. I realised that it could happen to anyone! But I could not stop drinking and in the end I found myself on a park bench, the lowest moment of my life, with nowhere else to go.

The kids were with friends, and I was alone. The sense of loss was overwhelming. Loss of family, friends, self-esteem; I'd lost the lot.'

In 1977, Pat walked into the Coolibah Centre at the Brotherhood. 'I had nothing, not even bread to eat. The two contact workers I met were very good to me, and not only did I get the food I needed to survive, but their care and concern taught me about "social action". I realised that I had a passion for it as well. I was soon employed to help with emergency aid and assisting people on the dole. I wouldn't take any money, because I hate money and what it does to you. I helped to find accommodation for people, and offered my time for volunteer work too. My kids went onto the children's program; the staff picked us up and respected us, we were never judged.

'My daughter Nicole had been fostered out at six months, to a family in New South Wales who really cared for her. When she was seventeen, she looked me up and wanted to establish a relationship; I was tickled pink about that. But it was short-lived. When Nicole was nineteen she went to a nightclub in Epping, where she was assaulted and murdered. We never found the body, although the bloke who did it said he dumped her remains somewhere at Kinglake. I was shattered, and my only wish is that someone will

> 'The sense of loss was overwhelming. Loss of family, friends, self-esteem; I'd lost the lot.'

find her so that she can be at peace. She had a very sheltered life and was naïve.

'The Brotherhood has been good to me, in friendship, in helping me at times to stay above the poverty line, in giving me a place to be and to help. Things are so different now. So many more people to look after, and the needs are so different: you could get by then, you can't now. And there are so many refugees as well; the focus of care has changed.'

Pat's connection here has, she believes, given her a rich life where the things that count the most – people – are indeed what matter. When she was in need, there were no women's refuges and she had to take pot luck, hoping someone would take her in. 'I mean, they are never judgemental and friendships are really important here. Those who work here help and direct; they listen and they are compassionate. I know people who have had opportunities for work opened to them; the Brotherhood has been a voice for so many people. Their social action is genuine because they are in touch with the nitty-gritty of the real world.

'I was once taken to a conference in Canberra to talk to the bigwigs. There were lavish rooms and food – stuff I don't care for much. They listened to me about things like the importance of everyone having a right to dental care and many other issues. I told the truth, and I was glad I did! I said what I believed.'

Pat Parker cares enough about people around her that her

involvement with the Brotherhood extends way beyond being a member of the Coolibah. She is a listener, someone who cares and who shares in the stories not only of the people we care for but also of the staff. She is honest, loving and down-to-earth, and has a generous heart and a good sense of humour; she believes in justice for all, no matter who. Her journey has not been so much remarkable as honest; here, at the place that responded to her needs, we are fortunate to be able to continue to draw on her wisdom and her special gifts. She represents several generations of people who have passed through and broadened the spirit of this organisation, and she has made us real and grounded in our work and encounters each day.

Andrew **Pearson**

In my years as a chaplain I have observed all sorts of people. One thing that I have seen in creative people is a particular skill in engaging with the world. They often have an ability to observe the details that support and bring life to everything – light, sound, smell, movement, even touch. Creative people often go into overdrive wondering how to capture the moment.

Andrew Pearson is a creative person who is trapped in the disease called Huntington's, an inherited neurodegenerative condition which destroys the brain cells that affect our emotions, intellect and movement. People living with this condition experience uncontrollable movements of the limbs, torso and face, and loss of mental abilities. They may also experience behavioural and personality changes. The symptoms are progressive and usually appear between the ages of 35 and 45. Huntington's affects each person differently.

These facts are important in order to understand something of what is so remarkable about Andrew. While he displays all the characteristic symptoms of the disease, he has a rare quality which is displayed through his enduring positive energy, through his hope, and through the gift of creativity.

Before he contracted Huntington's, Andrew studied art and design at Prahran College (now Swinbourne University) in Melbourne, majoring in graphic design, illustration and drawing. He also had a side interest in sculpture. His design career spanned 20 years and his talents were recognised and rewarded. He did everything from graphics for T-shirts to set design, costumes and props for the Brisbane Theatre Company. Andrew had moved to Brisbane after a romantic break-up because he had heard that it was a 'happening place'. While there he also worked with the state education department as an art director in illustration, film and video. His career path was highly creative and interesting.

Andrew began to develop the symptoms of Huntington's at the age of about 40. As the symptoms developed he lost his job because the pace was too fast. After being laid off, he felt devastated. At the same time his personal life was also hit hard: his first marriage had ended in divorce and his second wife 'came out' and then left him so she could live as a gay person. The combination of work and home troubles hit Andrew's sense of self and left him feeling shattered.

'I was lucky to find a deep and enduring friendship with Jane, who I met through my second wife. She recognises my needs and my wish to be close to my family; I adore her and she is the most important person in my life. She still lives in Brisbane, so I travel up and down to stay with her and to catch up with my strong friendship network up north.'

You see from Andrew's openness and friendly disposition that his positive attitude defies the march and progression of the disease. Angela, his support worker, comments, 'He's a special and generous person and I'm glad that I can be here to take care of him, to help with his particular needs and monitoring, but today I have a heavy heart because I need

'I know I will never beat the disease . . . but the more I am around creative people, the better my life is.'

to tell him that I am moving jobs. I feel devastated and emotional about this, and I want to tell him that he will always remain my great inspiration.'

Andrew is more philosophical: he has had other workers before Angela and, as appreciative as he is of her kindness, he knows that moving from one care-giver to another is an inevitable part of life for him. 'I know I will never beat the disease, but it is a fact that the more positive energy I can extend outward, the more connected and involved in creative pursuits I can be; and the more I am around creative people, the better my life is. It actually helps not only physically but emotionally as well. Engagement seems to be the key in wrestling with my symptoms.'

Angela comments, 'He helps himself tremendously by his

attitude. He has accepted things and been proactive, and has made all the necessary adjustments. He has lost a huge amount, and has had to develop a new life for himself. I think he is very brave.' Andrew brings life and hope to many people at the Banksia Centre, a day-care centre run by the Brotherhood of St Laurence in Carrum Downs, just south of Melbourne. His positive disposition, and his encouragement of those who attend the centre (many of whom suffer from dementia and acquired brain injuries), are a testament to the importance of continued engagement in life through friendship, networking and personal interests, and mental stimulation through reading and games.

'The disease itself has become a cause of fascination for me. I'm an avid reader of *New Scientist* and a gatherer of information from other sources as well. I'm particularly interested in stem-cell research – just take a look at me and you might be more inclined to say yes to it! I'm particularly interested in the latest theories on 'pre-aversion' therapy, where a chemical switches on the cell and genetically manipulates the gene. There is a lot of research happening and for me that brings a lot of hope.'

Andrew still makes some art. He draws 'goddesses' and has quite a collection. He uses different mediums – pastel, crayon and pencil. The work is precise and almost contradicts his involuntary movements and restlessness; you can see the real effort in the drawings. He does art classes at the Kingston Centre on Mondays where there is a Men's Society and through his care worker he was networked into Banksia.

'One thing that I really need is for people to listen to me when I'm down, and there are some things that I get really down about! I get frustrated by my loss of memory and sometimes I get so angry about it that I have an outburst. Part of the frustration is due to the fact that I can notice the changes in myself, which I find really hard to deal with sometimes. But it's not all bad. My friends mean a huge amount to me, not unlike most people, I guess. It's my friends, interests and activities that keep me involved and stimulated, and make life compelling. I don't have any children, but given what I know about the genetics of the disease I would say, reluctantly, that I suppose that's a blessing.'

'It's my friends, interests and activities that keep me involved and stimulated, and make life compelling.'

When I speak to others who know Andrew, I realise that there are plenty of people willing to listen. He's much liked, despite the awkwardness caused by his involuntary movements, which also cause him difficulty in speech and communication. But he still manages an affectionate and endearing laugh, which says that he is both trying hard and is grateful for the encounter.

We finish the interview and I can't help rising to my feet to give Andrew a hug. Angela has tears in her eyes. We retire to the activities room, where his friends are sitting around the edge of the room watching a game of shuffle. Ever the party boy, Andrew is greeted like a long-lost friend: 'Where have you been?' At Andrew's response – 'I've been interviewed for a book!' – there are noises and signs of acknowledgement and approval all round. Everyone reckons that if ever anyone deserved to have their story published, it's brave and courageous Andrew.

Anthony
Brennan

As a boy Anthony Brennan was, for various reasons, picked on at school, and though he enjoyed athletics and footy, every school day was a struggle for him. Despite the bullying, he enjoyed a secure, buoyant family life, which was a saving grace and a source of confidence for him. He did have a circle of friends: mates he knocked around with, riding skateboards and doing all the things kids get up to – including plenty of mischief! Some of those characters are still part of his circle of friends today.

Born in Melbourne in 1974, to Caroline and Rodney, Anthony Brennan spent his early years, along with brother Warwick and sister Jaclyn, in Rosebud. When he was six, the family moved to Frankston. One of his enduring mates, Paul, saw this new kid on the block: 'He came across the street, and gave me the finger and walked off. I told my father and we went across to see what was up. Paul said, "Just welcoming you to the neighbourhood and want to be your mate". He still is!'

Anthony's dad was a firefighter, and his mum stayed at home to look after the kids. He attended Canonook Primary School in Frankston and things went reasonably well until he was in grade 5 or 6. Poor eyesight and having to wear glasses, along with not having the benefit of the latest 'trendy' clothes that his peers enjoyed, made him the object of taunts and bullying, and school became a chore. But he stuck at it and got on with his studies, eventually completing his VCE. Anthony's eyesight remained problematic, and today he has minimal sight in his left eye and only 50–80 per cent vision in his right.

Leaving school without much ambition Anthony, like many, drifted: he got jobs packaging and warehousing on and off, and painting with a mate. Then, at a time when he was on Centrelink benefits, he was offered a New Start allowance, which changed his life. 'It was a six-month training program in timberwork (that's what I like to call it – they call it woodwork) at the Brotherhood's Furniture Works training centre. I lasted the six months, was offered a twelve-month traineeship, and then got a three-year apprenticeship.

'That was in about 1996. I wanted to be a mechanic, but this came along and I enjoyed it. I stayed on in furniture assembly and cabinet-making, and went on to do a Certificate IV in Assessment and Training. I became a workplace assessor and trainer, teaching the skills I've learnt. It wasn't all plain sailing, but Tony,

Charmian, Matt and the others helped me through.' He speaks of his workmates like they're family.

Anthony's next big step was when he purchased a house of his own. 'It meant a mortgage and all the responsibilities that come with a house. Mum went guarantor, but twelve months later I was able to transfer the property into my own name. You don't muck around with a house: every pay went into the bank, even before I'd buy food for the cupboard.'

His sense of responsibility for his home is linked to two things. The first is his blossoming relationship with Rachel, who came into his life four years ago, and the announcement of their engagement twelve months ago. 'I met Rachel at work, here at Furniture Works. We fell in love on the job, like many people do in the workplace, and I was careful to be discreet about it. I told Tony and Charmian first, and then people began to find out as time went on. Rachel finished the course and moved on; we are now engaged – we couldn't live and work together! Bugger that!'

The other factor is the long relationship Anthony has built with Furniture Works, and the programs he benefited from all those years ago, which he now finds himself delivering for the benefit of a new generation. While he has all the basic duties of making sure stocks are up-to-date and keeping the factory in running order, and meeting with the work team in his capacity as supervisor, Anthony sees his role as something more important in the big picture. 'I'm a straight-shooter, and I like to see things down the line. I see something of myself sometimes as we are preparing to begin a new program, and the students arrive apprehensive, a little disinterested, even unreliable, and definitely not wanting to be challenged. People like to think their way is the only way, and as soon as we can break that attitude the quicker we can help them. It's not a negative thing – we can make it really positive. The frustration can be that we go to all the trouble of setting things up for a new intake, and on the first day no one turns up: all the work and time and effort and the things we look forward to delivering – they fall flat and we are left cooling our heels. It usually works out in the end, but it can be frustrating.'

There is a sense that Anthony wants to make a difference in people's lives because a difference has been made in his life. It was only a few weeks before this interview that an encounter with an old school foe illustrated where he's at in the transformation of his life. One of his mates from school days brought a friend around to Anthony's house; he hadn't seen this guy since school, and his memories aren't particularly positive ones! 'He was really annoying at high school, and he came around with my mate to see what had become of me, and to see what my house might be like. He was blown away by what he saw and what I had achieved, and admitted that he didn't think that I would do anything with my life. It was a proud moment.

'I enjoy what I do, and even though at school I hated wood-work and wanted to be a mechanic, this job is satisfying. I'm doing things and have responsibilities that I never would have thought I'd have!'

You can see this in Anthony. There is almost a wisdom in his talk, which comes from his short but significant learning journey, and he is respected by the crew on the floor, including the students, because he is tough and firm yet self-effacing, and laughs at the ridiculous. Walking the floor at the factory, you see the change in these 'students' over time. At first they seem ter-rified by the new experience, perhaps because they simply lack confidence, having had no 'breaks' or opportunities in their lives. Or they may be picking up the pieces after things have gone horribly wrong in their lives – relationship breakdowns, loss of job and material assets, debt, injury – coming as they do out of a culture where hopelessness is an accepted norm and therefore what right have you got to dream? Some might think that it's their own problem or fault, that if only they'd get off their 'backsides' and do something they'd get ahead. But it's not like that. When you have had little support, little opportunity, even little love, getting a break seems almost impossible. Imagine what a life like that would do to the human spirit, and you can imagine what it's like for some of these people. Just walking the factory sometimes brings a tear to your eye.

At the Brotherhood, we often say that people who live in poverty, who struggle, have just the same dreams and aspirations as anyone else. Offering windows of opportunity is an irresistible challenge for a carer; Anthony, in working to transform others as he himself has been transformed, is a 'wounded healer'. It is as if he has found his vocation in life, which has in turn allowed him to aspire to those things which are everyone's right.

There is a lovely story Anthony tells, of going on a cruise in 1999 to New Guinea and the Solomon Islands, with his mates from school days. It was nothing like they had imagined: they had dreamt of bikini-clad women, the whole *Love Boat* deal, but instead the ship was full of elderly people on a Second World War remembrance tour. Yet they had a ball, because they ended up helping their fellow travellers, seeing the places that were important to them, observing their high emotions, and standing with them and listening to their stories . . .

'It really opened our eyes . . .'

You've done well, kid!

Beryl James

There is something of the larrikin in wild-haired Beryl James. She watches and observes everyone who passes by and provides the odd commentary – not always entirely complimentary. She is a little impatient at times, and calls a spade a shovel. But there is much more to this person than meets the eye, because for Beryl there are many things that matter very much, and her values are those from an earlier Melbourne, where neighbourhood and community were central to making sense of things and knowing that everyone would be all right in the end, even if they were struggling.

'We had good neighbours, and if you were in trouble you could go to them.' Beryl speaks of a tight-knit community where everyone helped each other and there were thousands of 'aunties'. She is quick to name the shopkeepers who lived down the street and looked out for her and her brothers and sisters when they were kids. They knew everything about everything and you respected them for it. But that all seems to be lost now, which as Beryl sees it is 'the heart of the matter with things now'.

Beryl has a story she loves to tell about her brother Ken, who recently passed away. 'He worked as a driver and drove a beautiful car, and one day I saw him in Bourke Street and whistled for him. This put the wind up a policeman, who came and questioned me; he said I couldn't afford a car like that, then asked if I knew the driver. I came straight back at him and said, "He's my brother!" The policeman backed off. That was the last time I saw my brother. He was my favourite – you could never keep him down and he was always restless, always off somewhere and doing something else.

'My parents, William John and Lillian Evelyn Martyn, lived in Coburg. There were three boys – Ken, Billy and Malcolm – a sister, and a girl they adopted, Lynette Joy.' Ken took off when he was just a lad and announced that he wouldn't return until he had a job. However, war broke out and Ken ended up serving in the Middle East. 'He was the best of the lot. All the boys enrolled: Billy went to New Guinea and Malcolm, who was much younger, got as far as Sydney but by the time he was accepted the war was over! He was that disappointed. Dad tried to enrol too but they just sent him home. Dad had been wounded in the First World War, and had lost an eye, so he didn't stand a chance.

'I got very sick as a child, with meningitis, and ended up in hospital in Fairfield for a long time.' This meant that Beryl's early schooling was interrupted and she only attended up to fourth grade. She later went to a 'girl's school' in Preston; because of her frail health, she spent much of her time learning domestic duties – particularly cooking, which she loved and developed as one of her passions. She has a large collection of cookbooks, which she often brings into the Coolibah Centre to show us; although she doesn't cook much these days, the books are still meaningful to her.

Though Beryl's sickness was severe, it didn't stop her getting up to all the things children got up to in those days. She was full of mischief, as were her brothers. 'Mum and Dad would go out to St Paul's in Coburg to play cards, which they loved, and Billy would be put in charge of us. We would cook, and stink the house out because we didn't open any doors or windows. Mum and Dad would come home to a terrible stench, but they never complained. If only they knew what we were getting up to!

'Dad was a postman, then later sat the big exam to become a customs officer; it was a very responsible job. Mum played tennis and was very good at it, but suffered from asthma, which slowed her down.' Beryl shows me some old photos of her mother when she was a child, which Beryl carries around with her. 'We would help out with the housework, and we liked to do that, it's what you did in those days. We would go dancing at the Brunswick Town Hall; old-time stuff. We would never go with the boys, because the place they went to was too rough, and Mum didn't want us going there.'

'I married the man down the street, and that was a mistake. He was on the bottle and it was "outa hand", so it didn't last very long – only nine months.' After Beryl left school, like many women of her generation she gained employment in an inner-city factory. Her task was to quality-test spray cans to make sure they worked. 'Fly spray, hair spray, they all came out of the same factory. (It belonged to Ensign's). One night the factory blew up, and spray cans were found for miles around for days after.' But mostly work was bits and pieces; there wasn't much to do. After the marriage she had few resources, and her family had gone their separate ways.

Beryl lived in many places around Melbourne, including cheap rented accommodation in Port Melbourne, where she was happy because it was close to the water. 'You would go down to see the ships coming in, and it was close to the tram, so the city was accessible. The house wasn't great, but I liked living there and it was only 80 dollars a fortnight. I was there for ten years, but then the owners sold it and I had to move out. I went back to Coburg for a short time, and I was happy being back in the north – closer to the family and the places I knew. It was familiar.

'But the family grew apart, and I don't see them now. Ken was the closest, and he's dead. The others weren't interested in looking after me and I wasn't going to look after them if they weren't interested! In our street when we were kids, there were mostly boys but there were five of us girls and we got away with a lot. That was Blair Street in Coburg. Friends make the difference to everybody – without them, there is nothing. They were good days.

'Sometimes we would see Grandma in Nicholson Street, taking her veggies down to the market to sell. Her house was large and backed onto a dairy in Preston, near Oakover Road. She had the benefit of the dairy cows' manure, and her pumpkins were so big it sometimes took two people to lift them.'

Beryl is a long-time member of the Coolibah Centre. She was introduced by a friend, Phyllis McGrath, who was connected with the Brotherhood. Quite simply, for Beryl it's somewhere to go and she's there most days of the week.

'I meet a lot of people here, even though I try to keep to myself and I do get into trouble at times because of my quick tongue. I call a spade a shovel. Living on my own in North Melbourne I do get lonely and I have little breakdowns occasionally, but that's because I'm alone. I've got two dogs, Boofy and Bobbie; I had another, but it died recently. The unit is quite big for me and it's a Housing Commission unit. I miss Port Melbourne because of the water and I prefer to be back in the north in the area I know well, but I have the Coolibah and even though I can upset people, I like being here and everyone knows me.'

As tough as Beryl is, she reminds me, as do many people like her, that connectedness gives us life and I wonder if, when he opened the doors of the Coolibah in the 1940s, Father Tucker had this in mind. Beryl also reminds me of the many personalities that make up a great city – when you hear how she feels that Melbourne has always been hers, it makes you think about our engagement with place and the part we all have to play in the responsible stewardship of our community. Beryl unwittingly highlights all these things, as a citizen and as a real member of the community of Melbourne. There is a justice issue here too and I would go as far as to say that Beryl is entitled to all the benefits, the spaces and the beauty of this city and its environs because, like us all, she has helped to create it. It's not about buildings, it's about people.

'It's all about friendship and that means everything!'

Carmelita
Rajahpakse

I remember years ago doing a short stint north of Melbourne in the Craigieburn-Dallas area. I would visit as many residents as I could to listen to them about their needs. Formerly a farming community, it was a new and burgeoning district and I was struck then by the sense of isolation that many people felt owing to the lack of infrastructure and transport, and social isolation as the result of the ethnic mix there.

In addition, many people had become weighed down with debt, having been persuaded to buy consumer goods on credit that were mostly beyond their reach. Often, husbands and wives would have to work double shifts to pay off these loans.

Outer suburban areas such as this can still be places of isolation, even though the infrastructure has improved. Carmelita Rajahpakse arrived in Australia from Sri Lanka to take up permanent residency in 2004. She had travelled to Australia many times to see her family, including her parents who had come to

Australia some years earlier, and while she knew that this was a move she had to make, her sense of isolation at first overshadowed the benefits of being reunited with her family.

'For my entire life my focus had been to work for the welfare of my village; I have a strong sense of community. In our culture, children are very important and family comes first. I came from a family of five children and I grew up under the fine education of the Carmelite Sisters who taught us the importance of looking after our young ones and that good leadership begins by helping at home.

'My focus has always been very much on young people and developing holistic welfare and activity opportunities for them, such as sport, language development and nutrition. I worked to make sure that surrounding villages had the sorts of resources that would nurture young people as they grew up.

'Building, clearing land and growing food were very important basic activities that needed to be organised, but so too was it important to bring villages together for things like annual sports meetings. It was about ensuring not only building a sense of community but also breaking down cultural barriers and indifference. Sri Lanka is such a beautiful place, but civil war is all that many generations have known and it still goes on. It was becoming difficult even for my son to visit us because he was concerned for the safety of his children and we simply couldn't risk their lives.

'I speak three languages – Singhalese, Tamil and English – which has been very helpful in the sort of community work that I love to do. I was taught by both family and the nuns that at the heart of the matter was not race, creed or colour but the human spirit, and I'm so thankful for that lesson. By believing there are no differences between people we can allow ourselves to be one big family. Beauty and colour are only skin-deep, but it is hard in a diverse land to keep the peace. I have always remembered that whatever we do, we do for the sake of our children so that they will have a future.'

Carmelita has a great love of gardening, which kept her sane when she first arrived in Melbourne. As she settled in her daughter's home she would do what many newly arrived immigrants do – simply wait for her family to come home each night, which made for a very long day and exacerbated her longing to be doing the things she knew and loved in her homeland.

She was told about a course being offered at the Craigieburn Family Day Care Centre under the auspices of the Brotherhood of St Laurence – a six-week training course in home care, under the direction of Eileen Buckley. So, at the age of 66, Carmelita did her Certificate 3 and Diploma in Children's Services and suddenly all the work she had once done has come back to her and given her life. She speaks highly of Eileen Buckley, a 'beautiful woman' and 'a godsend' who has enabled Carmelita not only to reconnect with community but to once again care for others.

'The course also challenged me to learn new ways of connecting with people and to develop my gifts in a safe and supportive environment. It makes me realise that at home I lived in tension all the time: we lost property, as we were constantly leaving things behind to move on somewhere else because of the strife, and life could be precarious. However, I will always feel that no matter where you are, your heart belongs in the place where you were born.

'Now I am giving to the community again, doing the sort of work that I did at home, in a new place. I work with an organisation that has the same values and offers the same life-giving links to communities in need that I had in my homeland. I still have immediate family responsibilities, as my mum is still alive and lives in Noble Park. My dad died a few years ago, when he was 97, and my husband died not so long ago, but both my son and daughter live here, so I'm close to my surviving family.'

Craigieburn Family Day Care Centre is a place of training for many people like Carmelita. On a training day there you can see something of the diversity of race and culture that is represented in the northern suburbs. Albeit isolated, Craigieburn grows ever closer to Melbourne as the urban sprawl continues and once-open paddocks are now covered with large Australian 'dream homes' that reflect a more materialistic generation. For those who built the Craigieburn of the 1960s and went without for many years, this adds to the challenge of reconciling the old world of the post-war 'baby boomers' and the new world of their children.

The arrival of people from different lands has brought a whole new dimension to the area, requiring us to think differently about the sorts of services and opportunities we might offer to this new generation. Carmelita and the many others like her are our new pioneers, forging a new sense of community.

Craig **Williams**

Those people who wonder whether or not a person who has little still harbours hopes and aspirations like the rest of us might find their answer in Craig's story. He does have one simple hope; that one day he might live in a government housing unit so that he feels he has a place of his own and some freedom to be himself. But there are other hopes and aspirations reflected in his story – which is that of a person who simply loves and has concern for others in need.

When Craig and his younger brother Peter were just little tackers, his parents split up and their father, Edward, took the boys from Queensland back to his home turf in Busselton, Western Australia, which was closer to his family and to an army base where he could work. Edward died of a heart attack when he was just twenty-five, having spent the last years of his brief life in and out of hospital. Craig and Peter were made wards of the state and their paternal grandparents ended up being their parents: Grandma became Mum to Craig, and he continues to hold her in deep affection.

Craig left school at the age of sixteen; he had been kept down

a year because he had a damaged his eardrum, and decided to get himself into the workforce. He gained employment as a medical orderly in Busselton Hospital and trained on the job to become an A-Grade orderly. He remained in this position for six years, then moved to Melbourne for a few years, living with an uncle and working at the Children's Hospital. He returned to Western Australia to look after his grandmother, who was in ill health, and while there he worked as a fish sorter at the fisheries warehouse.

Craig had a deep desire to reconnect with his birth mother and he started making inquiries through the Salvation Army. She was eventually located – she had remarried and was living in Rockhampton. Phone numbers were exchanged and Craig's mum finally called to set up a meeting, under the supervision of the Salvos. Here Craig met her for what was really the first memorable time; he also met her husband, and two half-brothers and a half-sister. During that meeting, Craig asked his mother why she had left them, but there was no reply. After the meeting, Craig went to Brisbane and got a job at a nursing home, waiting to hear from his mother again. Finally a call came from her, in which she told him that she wanted nothing more to do with him and would not see him again. That was that. Craig assumed it was because he had asked the question about her leaving, but he would never know. The conversation was over!

He returned to Melbourne in 1995 and gained employment

in aged care. But he damaged his back seriously and had to have several discs fused, which meant he could never do that sort of work again.

'I was passing by the Brotherhood of St Laurence one day, and saw a sign advertising membership at the Coolibah Centre, for people who were over 40, and I wandered in. I met Lori Anderson, who was the manager at the time, and she signed me up; I was attracted by the friendliness of people, who were kind and nice to talk to. We could play pool and chess and cards, and there was plenty of opportunity to have conversations, but there was also something quiet and peaceful about the place. We also went on camps and outings, and I helped to get the community garden going over at the Atherton Gardens housing estate in Fitzroy, as well as the garden out the back of the Coolibah. I joined the Coolibah members committee and really felt like part of the place, accepted.'

A new manager, Rod Miller, came to run the Coolibah; he saw potential in Craig, and perhaps concerned that someone of Craig's age was settling in too easily to passive pursuits, he introduced Craig to SecondBite, a not-for-profit program established in 2005 to collect and distribute surplus food to community groups and people in need. They were looking for a volunteer to drive and help out in the fast-growing initiative, which was right up Craig's alley. Suddenly he was thrust into the world of collecting fruit and veggies from markets, festivals, hotels and other institutions, and in so doing contributed to the human and friendly face of Second-Bite. His bosses love him and he loves the purposeful role he has, which he sees as providing real help to other people in hard circumstances. While he officially works only one day a week, he helps on the other days too and this has connected him with other activities, such as Meals on Wheels and street soup kitchens. He has come

'I like community and mateship, a close-knit society. It's important to me.'

to know many people – volunteers and those in need – in a very hands-on way. Craig's gift is his willing kindness and his enthusiasm for helping others, and this work has been a perfect match for him.

Personal networking is important for many people in Craig's walk of life, in order to remain safe and street-wise, and he is good at it. But he has also set certain standards, refusing to engage those who are into drugs. The network gives this community, both travellers and inner-city dwellers, a way of keeping an eye on each other so that they are safer than if they were going it alone. Many live in rooming-houses and are often exploited by their landlords or agents; their conditions are sometimes appalling.

Craig has good accommodation for the moment, at the Brotherhood's Sidney Myer House. He is grateful for that and happy with the group he lives with – Bernie, Martin and others – all good mates, all keeping an eye out for each other while they get on with their daily routine. He has lived in many other places in and around Melbourne, Brisbane and Perth, but for the time being he finds himself in the right place while still with a dream of having his own home one day.

'Living here,' he says, 'I come and go as I like. I have my own room and bathroom, and space and freedom. It's a place I can call home, and I don't have to worry about being chucked out! I like community and mateship, a close-knit society. It's important to me.'

Craig has casual work at Flemington Racecourse, which sees him quite busy during the state's Spring Racing Carnival in October and November each year. He is one of the gate people who checks visitors' tickets as they come through the turnstyles. 'You see some pretty funny sights on those days, Father Jeff!' He also does some head counting on trains to help determine the volume of commuters on Melbourne's transport system. These activities keep him busy and on the move.

Craig is a good person, with positive values and virtues. He can mix it with the best of them and taps quickly into most conversations, because he himself is interested in a lot of things. In his life he has been dependent on the goodness and charity of many people, and he rightly continues to remember and care for his grandmother, 'Mum'. Though denied the love of his real mother, he has found a path and – maybe through a certain innocence – got on with the journey responsibly, thoughtfully and, I would say, independently. Not to be outdone by anyone, he has engaged with the world in a wonderful way by simply being kind, and many people have benefited from that kindness. There are times of despondency, but Craig recognises the value of his community and his particular network of friends and supporters who he believes give him the courage and energy to get on with the day's tasks. He has a disarming smile, and is so respected at the Coolibah Centre that I think many see him as a friend and a carer rather than a member. Craig knows their names and they speak his with some delight, and will share a joke and a story with him. There is laughter, and contentment too, and there is home. He has become a son to many.

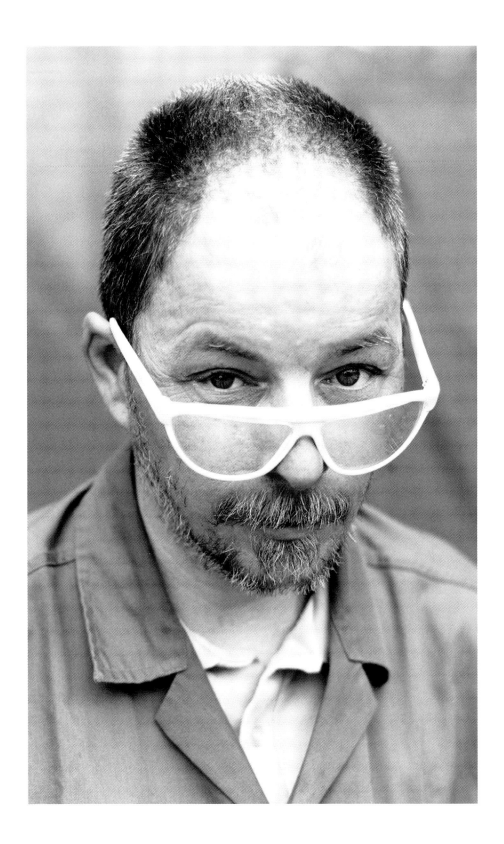

Darryl **Gardener**

You see Darryl making himself busy around the Coolibah Centre. He's an interesting-looking guy and wears a pair of white-framed glasses like, he says proudly, those worn by the character 'Brains' in the series *Thunderbirds*. They're a little too big for him; he says he found them in a shop, a bargain at 14 dollars, and had his own lenses fitted. Darryl loves to garden – in fact, it's a real passion and is what attracted him to the Coolibah Centre in the first place. He discovered the gardening project there when he was visiting one day; he has been a member ever since.

You will often see Darryl leaning on the rails around the garden conversing with somebody about what needs to be done or the latest planting. He plays a mean game of pool, although he's quick to tell you that he's not as good as he used to be. He enters into conversation easily and enthusiastically; there are a few issues that will push his buttons, and off he goes.

Darryl was born in East Melbourne in March 1960. His birth was a tough one: the doctor used forceps roughly, as the result of which he was born with brain damage which has also left him epileptic. 'But I've learnt to live with it.' The damage was identified immediately and Darryl's mother was told that it was so severe that the baby would best be put straight into a home.

'I lived in the boys' home because she couldn't look after me, because I was sick and my dad had taken off. In fact I only saw him once, when I was four years old, and even then he was drunk. Mum lived in Belgrave and I had a sister. Mum married when I was eight and my sister was five. Our stepfather was fantastic, a gentleman, and he was real good to us, did everything and more that a real father would do.

'The boy's home, in Burwood, was called Allenby. It had different sections with different names, and I went through all the sections because they were divided by age groups, from babies up to age six. But we would get a chance to play with each other. It wasn't a bad place; I felt looked after. Then I moved to Hillside in Wheelers Hill when I was seven, because I was too old for Allenby. Some of the kids didn't have families and some didn't have a good home. My family was good because they came to visit me a lot, so I had a sense of belonging. I played a lot of pool – I was so good at it it wasn't funny, much better than now. We went on lots of

> **'I lived in the boys' home because [Mum] couldn't look after me, because I was sick and my dad had taken off.'**

outings and I had some foster parents who were good to me. They would take me to the Eye and Ear Hospital every Thursday for speech therapy. There was little schooling for us and I really only spent time in school up to Year 7.

'I got a job working in a juice factory in Burwood when I was thirteen. I stayed at Hillside until I was eighteen or nineteen. When I was too old to live there any more I moved into a rooming house in Canterbury. I continued at the juice factory for fifteen years, until it closed down. Then I moved to the city, which didn't work: I was in that hotel on the corner of Spencer and Flinders Street and it was awful.'

There was a departure from the commentary at this point, as Darryl got very worked up about the hotel and asked me if I had ever been there. Strangely enough, I had been looking for somebody years ago and had come across the place. I was horrified that anything like it could exist in Melbourne – it was like stepping into the very worst of Victorian London – so it was easy to agree with Darryl's feelings. He talked about exposed electrical wiring, the fact that there were no fire extinguishers, how long-term tenants got sick. He had felt ripped off because of the squalor of the place, which the owners could get away with because it was privately owned. 'We don't do that to each other. Our Heavenly Father would be shocked.' He made the sign of the cross and put his hands together as though praying.

Luckily, one day Darryl ran into his sister in the city and she urged him to move home to be with his mum. He jumped at the chance. This was a very important time for him, because for other than occasional weekends he had never lived at home. For the next four years he was with his mother, he also found a job at a sheltered workshop in Broadmeadows, which had been set up for handicapped and disabled people, and there he 'packed stuff, and things like that'.

In this place he found Angela. It was love at first sight and they married in 1986. 'She's 4' 8" and she suffers from a syndrome that means she can't have babies. We do everything for each other and she is kind and thoughtful. When people meet her, they just want to sit and speak with her for ages.' Darryl and Angela live in a unit in Glenroy, which has a garden. At the moment Darryl has a big task in caring for Angela, as she has a brain tumour and is undergoing treatment at Peter MacCallum Cancer Centre. He assures me that he's enjoying good support and care from people and I believe this is true, but he is also a positive and optimistic person and is very gracious about those around him. His days at the Coolibah Centre are obviously important, giving him some space as well as contact with his friends, and giving Angela contact with hers. 'I also help other people when I'm here. It's really important that we help each other.'

When I asked Darryl what his hopes and dreams are for a

better world, his response was interesting though not really surprising. He believes he has helped make the world a better place and considers himself to be kind and thoughtful; he is keen to be an advocate for others, particularly in relation to accommodation problems; he's determined to sort out the issue at the hotel in Spencer Street. Then he shifted into a sort of confession. 'I used to do stupid things when I was in my twenties, like doing heavy drugs and smoking and drinking and speed and all that stuff. But I stopped in 1985 when I asked Angela for help. Our Heavenly Father helped me too and He helped Angela and guided her in the right way. But you have to make it work – you have to listen to what God wants you to do, and be open to it.'

'You have to make it work – you have to listen to what God wants you to do, and be open to it.'

There is a surprising twist at the end of our interview when Darryl mentions in passing that he fixes bikes for the needy. He started doing this through St Mary's House of Welcome, a day centre for homeless people in Fitzroy, and fixes them for the people in the Atherton Gardens flats. He can show you, as he says, 'the right way to fix a bike'. He actually converted an old column heater into a bicycle and he can occasionally be seen riding it up and down Brunswick Street.

It struck me during the interview that the opportunities, good support and encouragement he seems to have had as a child through the boys' homes, his attentive family and the generosity of his foster family have given Darryl a 'can-do' attitude to life. This seems in turn to give him an energy and a faith in himself, and he's not frightened to express his opinions. About the right to dignity of all people he's articulate and determined. Darryl wants to make a difference to people's lives, and in the places in which he engages, he certainly does.

Dave **Graham**

Dave Graham is a courageous soul who would like to do everything he can for himself, but because of various conditions from which he suffers he is unable to be fully independent, a fact that he has come to accept. He is not afraid to ask for help and assistance when he needs it. He has lived a difficult life that was determined by one event when he was a newborn baby, yet he has been able to develop a sense of living in the present. At the Brotherhood, he has found a place where he is able to discover new skills and relationships in a supportive and loving environment. His courage and tenacity are an inspiration to everyone.

Dave was born in Mordialloc in 1966. He was premature and needed close monitoring during the first days of his life. Sadly there was a moment when he was left alone in the birthing unit and he stopped breathing; the resulting severe lack of oxygen left him with acquired brain injury, which caused severe short-sightedness and epilepsy. His short-sightedness makes him attentive to the conversations that take place around him. And as he taps into other people's talk, he is quick to contribute his own opinions and observations.

Dave has a younger brother and sister. His mum Yvonne, with whom he lives, is his best mate. His father has not been part of the family for many years. 'I'm angry about my dad taking off and I feel that I've really missed out. I'm angry because I reckon that life has been really tough on Mum.' His father, deserting the family as he did, set in motion the events that would become Dave's life journey, a roller-coaster ride without a seat-belt! Dave reckons that his life has been 'sheer hell'.

'My mother had no option but to institutionalise me at the age of five. Imagine having to do that! The medication they made me take for my fits and stuff made me hyperactive, and Mum couldn't cope. The kinder would just send me home; I was out of control. They just could not cope with all the crap I got up to and the amount of energy I had. I used to get out of the house and just take off, and everyone would be searching for me. I was sick a lot and suffered from such high temperatures that they would put me in the car and drive me around the neighbourhood in the evenings to cool me down!

'My mother had no option but to institutionalise me at the age of five. Imagine having to do that!'

'I spent sixteen years at a children's home in Bundoora, where I got beatings from staff members. I would be tied to a bed and beaten black-and-blue, but I couldn't say anything because I was so scared of what would happen if I did.' The abuse he suffered is visible in his demeanour and there is a sense that he is still frightened by the memories of that terrible time. His mother feels great guilt and remorse for what happened to her son while he was out of her care, and for her sake he is careful not to go into too much detail.

When Dave was a child his mum would often swear and say, in sheer frustration, 'What have I done?' and apologise to Dave for all that he suffered. Dave loved and understood her enough to reassure her that he didn't believe it was her fault, that with his dad gone there was nothing much she could have done differently. He understands the predicament she was in at the time and feels no bitterness towards her.

Dave's story reflects the powerlessness that a family can experience, especially if they are dependent on public services and are stretched to the limit, unable to serve the needs of each individual family member. It is easy for everyone in a vulnerable family unit to become victims of neglect at many levels.

'I still suffer from feelings of hurt and abuse because Dad pissed off. I have seizures, some of them so bad that I have suffered some permanent memory loss.'

Dave has a great sense of humour. Recently, at a staff meeting in our Frankston office, we invited him to talk about his life and his connection with the Brotherhood of St Laurence. Overcome with nerves and excitement, he began by offering some critical as well as positive reflections about the other speakers who had gone before him. He then realised what he had done – he'd given some handy speaking hints to the Executive Director and a range of industry experts! He did not hesitate to send himself up as well, for good measure.

Dave talked about the transformation he had undergone over the previous twelve months. He described how it felt to find an organisation where his needs were understood, to be among people who took him seriously, to become a meaningful participant in an organisation that seeks to help people who have struggled through life.

Through the Brotherhood, Dave has learned some important life skills, which have instilled in him a sense of responsibility and commitment to the needs of others, giving his life added meaning. He has learned practical skills as well – proudly telling us that he has a newly acquired computer at home – which have enabled him to take on volunteer work at the Brotherhood and to help around the office, taking telephone calls; he's a joker, making the girls laugh. This involvement and the development of meaningful relationships beyond his family and small support group has built his confidence and added a distinctive and enjoyable dimension to his life.

Recently, after we had been talking, he was determined to

find his own way back to the Brotherhood office, which was a kilometre down the road. He would be travelling in unfamiliar territory, but his sense of independence and adventure is such that he would not be persuaded to accept a lift. Twenty minutes later, as I was about to drive off, I saw Dave trying to climb over the cyclone-wire fence on the adjacent property – he had managed, in that time, to walk full circle and arrive back where he had started. We retrieved him and he politely asked whether we might give him a lift back to the office after all. He was independent, but did not fear asking for help if things did not work out. We could all learn from this sensible humility.

Elvie Brown

'You know, there is no need to be lonely. I'm alone, but I'm never lonely; I'm living life, and I have the clouds and the blue sky and the garden and the wind. Carers and Meals on Wheels come and go every day, and visitors too. My life is full, and it is good.'

Elvie's home is neat and well ordered; everything has a place. Today she is expecting me and she has done some considered thinking about what she might like me to take away from our conversation. I imagine that she has run some ideas past other people who have seen her that day. I'm fifteen minutes late, so there is a gentle ticking-off, but that also gives Elvie the opportunity to offer me some insight into the sort of person she is and what she might expect from someone who makes an appointment to speak with her!

I settle in. There is a chair for me to sit facing her so that we are focused, and around her are the things she will refer to, as we talk; from objects she has collected and been given over the years to a standard boxing ball in the corner, which she uses every day to strengthen her arms and improve her co-ordination.

Elvie's opening comments set the scene, and we are away.

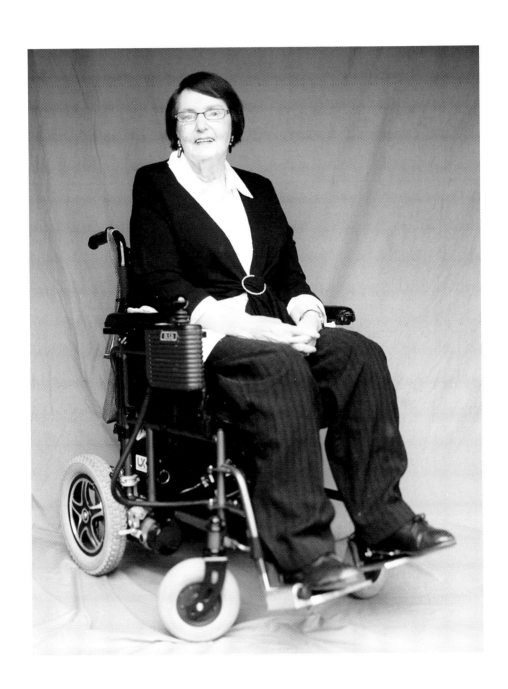

'I'm a talker, and enjoy good conversation!' Living with dignity is central to her talk, her presence, her home; she is a dignified person. 'I believe in euthanasia. I have put things in order and I want to go out with dignity. There are too many people in the world, and not enough carers.' This seems to be the heart of Elvie's dilemma. She has no desire to be a burden to anyone.

It seems to me that the way in which Elvie has arranged her home environment is designed to show the visitor that there is order and purpose in her life. She did go to a nursing home to see what it would be like to live like that. 'I went as an observer, and I didn't like what I saw . . . I haven't got much time for those who just go and lie down to die.' I venture to suggest that we don't stop living until we are dead. Elvie agrees: 'Never say never.'

> 'I'm alone, but I'm never lonely; I have the clouds and the blue sky and the garden and the wind.'

Elvie has a daughter, Dorrell, who is married, and two grandchildren: Rachel-Lee, who is 34, and James who is 30. The unit is full of pictures of the family.

Her focus seems to be strongly on the management of her physical and medical problems, not so much in a self-centred way but rather with the aim of managing her needs so that she is on top of the issue. To let go, it seems, would to her mean defeat, the thought of others taking over and managing her – and she is not ready for this.

Elvie has multiple sclerosis, which was diagnosed in 1960. 'I have been an active person all of my life, and since the diagnosis I've worked hard for much of the time to combat the disease. I can't walk now. I was on a stick at first, really just to let people know to be careful; I progressed to crutches and then, as you see, to a wheelchair. I can't bear my own weight at all, so I'm confined to this. But I do have a high pain tolerance.' The boxing ball is part of combating the disease. She copes well and is proud of it, but she is also aware of her own frustrations, she would like to be able to do more. That's why her ordered home is important; and keeping busy and having visitors and going out – human contact – helps her to be content.

Elvie has been married twice. Her first husband, Frank, was a keen cricketer and would have made the Test team if it wasn't for the outbreak of the Second World War; he played for North Melbourne after the war. He was with Intelligence during the war, later working for the Department of Supply and Defence. 'Our marriage failed. We didn't get along, and he was a gambler; we divorced and later he died of a heart attack.' Her second marriage was to Rodney William Brown, who was 'a bricklayer, a good dancer, and a good provider. He was meticulous and selfish.' Rodney didn't cope with Elvie's diagnosis, and became an alcoholic, but he was also a 'war neurosis case'. Elvie remembers him as a serious fisher-man – he would travel to New Zealand or Albury to fish – 'and he also built beautiful houses'.

Elvie's connection to the Brotherhood came through her carers. District nurses and her case managers, Lisa Astete and Robert Woodruff (affectionately called 'Rough Nut'), picked up on her need to connect with people and to be active. Elvie joined an exercise class at Carrum Downs, and goes weekly to spend time with a special group of people who for many reasons come together to do movement and group games, to talk and to support one another under the direction of Adam, a fitness instructor who has run the program for more than ten years. Visiting the class gives me an opportunity to see what is so special, and a little unusual, about the gathering. There is a lot of movement, with one-on-one attention and some group activities, with every-one taking part in a whole lot of options on the floor at once. It's like an unwieldy orchestra warming up for a spectacular moment, not with instruments but with wheelchairs and balls, walking sticks and hoops. Their movements are unselfconscious because, no matter what their ailments might be, for this moment in their week they seem free from all the hindrances of their disabilities. For all the cacophony of sounds and movement, it's a beautiful and liberated scene.

'You want to cry and laugh at the same time, and wasn't

it Dolly Parton who once said, "That's the best emotion of all!" Lovely.'

Elvie is also a keen and accomplished swimmer, and was once asked to join the Victorian swimming team for disabled people. She swam half a mile twice a week! She also goes target shooting and claims to be a good shot, always close to the bullseye.

Elvie was always active and she has plenty of stories of the many things she did and achieved in her younger, fitter days. She also lovingly remembers Melbourne in 'her day'. Child of the Depression years, she was born in Bell Street in Coburg, where her parents lived. When she was two the family moved because her mum and dad lost the house. They lived with an aunt in Malvern Road, and since then she has lived in 21 different places, including interstate, being settled in Frankston for the last 28 years. She remembers cable trams, and waiting for girl friends and boy friends under the clocks at Flinders Street Station. She left school at the age of thirteen, like many of her contemporaries, learnt a trade and became a dressmaker, which was 'seen as lowly work', in Hardware Lane off Little Bourke Street. Melbourne was so safe then.

'Mum was good at icing cakes and the baker would get her to do the icing for his supply. There were lovely shops, tea-rooms and tobacconists. I loved dancing, and went out nearly every night, to St Kilda, the Masonic Hall in Collins Street, and the Exhibition

Buildings. I had to rush to get the last train home. I spent eighteen months in bed with pleurisy and TB, and now realise they were probably early symptoms of MS.'

She has a break here because, as she says, 'The MS gives me delayed memory. I can picture what I want to say, I can say it in my head, but can't find the words. But I remember what to say some time later.'

Elvie's front door is always open for anyone to come and visit her and she is still talking as I leave after a few goodbyes. Miraculously, as I finally step out onto the front porch, another visitor appears to take my place and the conversation continues. Elvie's happy.

Elyse Maurelli

Elyse is strong, determined, imaginative and intelligent. At times her life is difficult, made worse by the strength of her personality, for she can bamboozle some people and confuse others. She often finds herself sitting in no-man's-land, as it were, having challenged her carers or her peers with bright intelligent words and somehow got them offside. Elyse, like all of us, has a story to tell. She has been a constant visitor and member of the Coolibah Centre for more than 20 years and her personality ensures that she is remembered by all who pass through the doors. She is a sassy dresser and you get the impression that every article of clothing, every bangle, necklace and earring, has been carefully chosen both to adorn a stunning woman and to tell us what sort of space she is inhabiting at that moment.

'Things weren't very good in Europe, so in October 1938 we left to come to Australia. My schooling was under the aegis of the Freemasons, where my father was a Past Master [a former senior officer]. I gained scholarships to Mac.Robertson Girls' High School and Melbourne University, which I left in second year. I had no choice, as my father died and my bursary was relinquished.

'My childhood had not been easy. At the age of eleven I came home from school one day to find that my mother, for eight shillings a week, had made my sister and me wards of the state. I was described as an 'uncontrollable delinquent' and spent time in many different homes; the least I can say is that it was not nice. I've always been afraid since then of females in double-breasted jackets with manifests under their arms!

'I came home from school one day to find that my mother, for eight shillings a week, had made my sister and me wards of the state.'

'When I left uni I decided I would go to sea as a merchant seaperson. I travelled around the Australian coast and on a coal burner to Nauru, and went to New Guinea. When I was ashore I studied hospitality through the William Angliss College, with a focus on hospitality administration. I was sent by the Australian Wine and Brandy Association to do a course in London, and for many years I swapped between going to sea and working onshore.

'I think many of us have watershed moments in our lives. Mine was in 1970, when I was involved in a terrible car accident: a single-car roll-over in which my husband, and my son aged seven and a half months, were killed. I went under the bed for nearly two years with a serious nervous breakdown; I could not function.

Then I found the Brotherhood of St Laurence, and the organisation and the people in it became my saviours and my solace. Whenever I was in Melbourne and not travelling, I was totally involved with the Brotherhood. I helped them by working as a volunteer in various op shops and doing administration work.

'I'm really pleased to say that things are going well at this moment in my life. Six months ago I had an operation to give me two titanium discs in my spine and the surgeon promised me I wouldn't be on a walking frame or in a wheelchair. And I'm not: I'm going very well now. I can go on trains, planes and buses, and drive a vehicle. I like to know that I can be on the move!

'The Coolibah Centre is still my support; I am here daily. I love to have a cup of tea with my friends in the afternoon, and I love to be with my particular friend Monty for breakfast in the mornings. He hasn't been well at all lately and that bothers me. The things he used to do were amazing. He collected for various hospitals – we're talking thousands of dollars – but he's not capable of doing that at the moment. He used to shake tins at the Victoria Market, go to the gym, go to work. He's a workaholic, so being unable to do these things is badgering him. He's not aware that his physical disability will go on for some time. I try to bolster his spirits as best I can, to keep him on a level plane, to help him accept the things he cannot do and realise that it will be some time before he may be able to do them again.

'Monty James, real name Maurice John James, is unsighted. I'm glad to have been a friend and mentor to him for 25-odd years. He lives in a rooming hose in Gertrude Street in Fitzroy. Monty is a very strong character, which is why he's not coping very well with the things he's not able to do at the moment. However, he has a lot of care and I love him dearly.

'In the Coolibah we have people from many cultures mixing together and to my mind we care for each other respectfully, with compassion and concern.'

'Needless to say, after all these years I've seen a fair amount of change at the Coolibah – many managers, many chaplains, many priests. I'm still a friend of Dr Peter Hollingworth [Executive Director of the Brotherhood from 1980 to 1991]; I can go and have a cup of tea with him any time. I've been to China six or seven times over the years. When I used to travel there, I was a card-carrying communist, which led me to Cuba, Tibet, Bhutan, right through Russia and to various other places. Through that experience I have come to understand the cultures of Asia very well. In the Coolibah we have the pressure of people from many cultures mixing together – people from Germany, Greece, Poland and Asia – and to my mind we care for each other respectfully, with compassion and concern. Many of us are not very agile, considering the ageing process! We look after each other well.'

I like to think of Elyse's friendship with Monty, through whom she has been able to channel much genuine feeling and loving care. Recently Monty died. Elyse, with great courage, stood to tell all of us at the Coolibah Centre something of his story, and she did great justice and honour to his life. Her volunteer work at the Brotherhood has been significant and energetic. Her consistent and practical love for Monty has taught all of us what it means to be a real friend.

Gilbert (Gil) Baker

'I stole my older brother's birth certificate so I could go to the Vietnam War. I was there for nine months in 1966-67; my mate Rodney lost his left eye. After I got back I got done by the authorities because I had falsified my age. I got fined and was denied the service medal as punishment for what I had done. But at least I got paid!

'I was born behind the old Ballarat brewery in 1945, in the house on top of the hill. Nineteen people lived in that house and on the verandah. I was born in the barn. The house is still there and is now a hostel. When my mum and dad died we scattered their ashes in Lake Wendoree.

'I'm Indigenous, because mum was an Aboriginal. She was born on Kangaroo Island off the coast of South Australia. Dad had a bit of Yank and Irish in him and they met during the Second World War while Dad was based at Ballarat. Mum had moved across to the mainland and was helping out at the settlement. They got married and had nine children and I'm number six.

'We had no TV, not even fishing rods. We would just grab a stick and a wire and go fishing; that was our sustenance and our entertainment. We had a great childhood. We found the back way into the brewery, got to know the train driver and would hitch rides; we'd fish, hunt kangaroos and rabbits, and we would go for long runs – bare-foot, because if you want to become an elder or a tracker or a warrior you need strength in your footwork. Cathy Freeman trained barefoot. It makes the soles of your feet harder and it's easier to climb hills. We just used to wear a kangaroo- or rabbit-skin cloth, as little clothing as possible.'

Gil has acquired brain damage, the result of a brutal assault two or three years ago. Police witnessed the attack and someone even filmed the incident. The local bus had pulled up at the front of his house and Gil had gone out to help his wife with the shopping, when a car pulled up behind the bus and some youths jumped out with a shovel and other things. That's all he can remember. His three-year-old daughter was attacked and his wife assaulted. Gil ended up in intensive care: as well as suffering brain damage, he had six broken ribs, neck injuries, a perforated eardrum, his nose was broken and there was a 75-mm hole in his skull. He has lost confidence, suffers physically and lives with severe loss of memory.

Before the assault Gil was fit, outgoing and confident. He

deals not only with his own trauma but with a suffering family: a wife who is very shaken up; his young daughter, Chloe, coping with counselling and other help; and his son, Adam, who witnessed the whole thing and was deeply affected by it. In recent times Gil has injured his back by pushing himself too hard, but he has found the Brotherhood and it has become his second home, where he has a vital role as a volunteer. For him this is a place of respite, but it is also a place that challenges him to actively face his demons and reconnect with and trust people. He has stood up publicly to tell his story, and this took a great deal of courage.

Gil has a glint in his eye, which makes you think that he has both hope and some stories to tell.

Gil has a glint in his eye, which makes you think that he has both hope and some stories to tell. This guy is no saint; in fact, larrikin would be an apt description. While acknowledging the gravity of what he has been through recently, you can delight in his familiar story – that of a young Australian growing up in the 1950s and 1960s, with few resources but enough imagination to get himself into healthy trouble.

'On my sixteenth birthday I was broke, and I pinched a railway maintenance engine and took it from Glen Waverley to Richmond – with assistance on the way from the guards at the level crossings. I knew I'd get into deep trouble – but it didn't bother me too much.

'I was a hell-raiser. Me and me mates would build billycarts and have races. When we lived in Caulfield, the council would help set up a track for us and the police used to come to stop the traffic. The local kids would be at the bottom of the hill screaming for the billycart to reach them.

'It was always good to do the paper run for Mr Hill. His was the first paper shop to have children deliver and sell papers; they'd be paid five pounds for a week's work. And because Toppa Ice Cream was situated nearby in Warragul Road, the kids would vie for position to deliver papers to the company so you would get a free ice-cream. They were great times.

'Because we lived in Caulfield and not far from the race track, I dreamed of being a jockey, but I was too big so I became a stable-hand, cleaning up the stables and tending the horses. On race day I'd polish the harnesses and equipment so that the horses were properly prepared. Once my work was done and the races were on I'd go swimming in the ponds and sometimes sleep in the empty stalls.

'As kids we would put together our own cricket bats and make footballs out of old pairs of socks. But we managed to get hold of three good footballs by going to watch St Kilda at Junction Oval: the goals were so close to the fence that when the balls went over we would grab them and make a run for it.'

Gil started a music group called 'Springy Rock', which turned out to be very successful. 'We would meet at the Springvale Town Hall and people would come from all over Melbourne. The band and the dancing went for years, and gained the attention of people like Molly Meldrum, Jon English, Frankie J. Holden, Johnny O'Keefe (who became a mate) and many others. The concept was so successful that seventeen other clubs opened up around Melbourne.

'My mates Rodney, Len and myself used to light bonfires in a paddock where the Matthew Flinders Hotel is now. There was no great danger, but fires would break out and the police and fire-fighters would know it was 'the boys'. The punishment wasn't so bad – we just had to clean fire trucks. The Catholic Church's Don Bosco Home, for difficult boys, agreed to take us in. Father Baker would make me pray for God's forgiveness, but he also taught us boxing and, strangely enough, boomerang throwing.'

> . . . he offers to others what he might wish for himself, and does so with the sensitivity that is essential in caring for people of such frailty.

As much as there's a glint in his eye, Gil is kindly, patient and a very good listener, and his volunteer work at the Brotherhood assists the paid workers in offering the practical and even spiritual care that members require. You see Gil guiding and helping visitors with activities as well as basic toileting needs and just finding their way around. He knows their stories and their limitations, and is able to offer some challenge to stretch their abilities. It could be that he offers to others what he might wish for himself, and does so with the sensitivity that is essential in caring for people of such frailty.

While I wasn't entirely surprised by Gil's Indigenous heritage, as he told his story I was reminded of the depth of Indigenous connectedness with the land. His running barefoot wasn't only about toughening the soles of the feet but also about the human soul connecting with the earth. His delight in the world he now knows helps him see that his own life still has great purpose; in his trauma he has come to a deeper compassion for those who suffer – often in silence – from not being independent or even fully alive. You see, in the faces of those who suffer from dementia, and sometimes acquired brain injuries, a longing to be released from the strange place in which they find themselves. One person can add something to their lives by helping them connect with the simple and the complex, which make all things make sense. Gil is one of these people; one who was helpless has become a significant helper.

Jeffrey Robertson

Jeff was born in November 1955 in Redfern in Sydney, one of a large Catholic family. He talks about 'the Block', that part of the suburb where Aborigines congregated to live and which became a community of the very poor, the destitute and the discriminated-against. 'We were on the edge of that area, which took in everything from one side of Redfern Station across to Chippendale. I grew up in a world where you had to do what you were told or you got slapped, and it didn't do us any harm. I had three sisters and two brothers; one brother died from rheumatic fever, and one sister drowned when she was seven.'

Both Jeff's parents worked, so the kids had particular household chores to do. 'Dad was very strict: there was trouble if Mum's bath wasn't drawn and the tea wasn't on the table when they got home. Because they weren't around during the day, our family life was dysfunctional and aggressive; that's what Redfern was like for all of us. But you were taught to accept all people regardless of

colour, race and creed. Mum was a Roman Catholic, though, and you know how they responded to some things: homosexuality was not tolerated, because they were seen as sick and perverted; and if you got someone pregnant, you married them. That was my culture, macho and strong, and it stuck with me for many years. In our world there was no room for the weak; it was the survival of the fittest. We had to live with what we had and that created a lot of different issues; many kids had to steal food so they had something to eat at school. This wasn't our habit, because we didn't need to, but we lived through traumatic times – like my sister dying when I was fourteen, and within a year I was raped at gunpoint by a friend of the family, who had raped other members of my family. I married at eighteen, because I got a woman pregnant and Dad said I had to. We had another child by the time I was 21.

'I got a job as an apprentice chef because that's what I love to do. But soon after our second child was born, my wife left – she wanted to see the world, so she shot through. I was a single parent for the next few years, which deepened my relationship with the children. When I was 29 my wife came back; she remarried, and amicably took custody of the children. With no family responsibilities I had the opportunity to begin my own travels, so for the next eleven years I travelled through France, Italy and Holland, to China and the islands, working. I felt reassured that the kids' stepfather was looking after them well. I got a job at Maxim's in Paris, which gave me confidence that I was good at what I did; the cooking my father had taught me – the old-fashioned stuff – had given me a good basis, particularly for French cooking. When I think of it, from the age of eight I would cook about 70 per cent of the meals for eight people each week at home, from roasts to crumbed brains, depending on the budget and the week. I loved it, but I had to because it was my job.

'The hardest workplace was in a restaurant in Beijing, where I learnt how to make yum cha. It was a physically hard existence and it was a sweatshop in every sense of the word, but it was their culture. The level of poverty was similar to Redfern, but the sense of community support and family commitment in China was educational: the way they looked after each other, and their respect for their elders, are so different to our way, and impressive; it makes me understand why they stick together in new countries where they come to live.

'My eleven years of travel was life-changing, exciting and lots of fun, and opened my eyes to the ways other communities live. I saw the same sorts of things in Italy and in France, the way in which people looked after each other in poorer areas by pooling resources.'

Jeff came back to Australia in the mid-1990s and settled in Sydney. 'I had a zip around Australia and caught up with the kids, now both adults and training to go into the police force in Western Australia. They were having a good life.' He moved to Tasmania for a while and there met his second wife, with whom he had two children, Samantha and Jonathan. Jeff became ill and assumed he had chronic fatigue syndrome, but after more tests he was found to be HIV-positive. 'All the past cultural stuff came to the fore. Homophobia, how people were dying of AIDS. It was a big shock. Tablets, panic, horrible feelings of insecurity. Does my family have it? Do we kill everyone because we are going to die anyway? My Christian wife was remarkably understanding, but gave me gloves to wear around the children!'

Jeffrey had to start on medication immediately, as he was carrying a 'high load' in his system; the virus had started taking over very quickly. He was hospitalised in 1998 and was told that he had two years to live. His wife took off with the kids and he later found out that they had been told he was dead. His mother couldn't cope; she was overcome with fear and ignorance about Jeff's plight. 'She just didn't want to know, and she made sure I always ate off the same plate!' To add to his grief and growing depression over his situation, Jeff's daughter was killed in a car accident and within months his mother died. He decided to end it all and came to Melbourne with a firm plan to kill himself.

'I drank, I became self-destructive, but I still took my medication and in doing so realised that I didn't want to die. I had become emotionally and physically bankrupt. The drinking was so heavy that they put me in a support house and diagnosed me with acquired brain damage, but later they recognised that I was having an HIV-related emotional breakdown. I was sent to Warrnambool to a rehab centre and given the opportunity to learn about the disease. Between 2000 and 2003, I got back my life.'

Jeff did a work-place training assessor's course, to help others but also to learn about himself. There was tension as he learnt to live with the bigotry of a small country community, where people were quick to accuse and judge him and hatred was expressed in graffiti and rumours. The whole town 'knew' that he had HIV, and soon he was being called a 'faggot' and a 'child molester'. The truth was that he had contracted HIV through a blood transfusion while in Europe. He made the monumental decision to stay and fight the bigotry and offer education to the people of the district to help them understand the disease. A further setback occurred in 2003 in the form of a stroke, HIV-related, and at the age of 47 he was sent to a nursing home.

'These were tough times. I was a "veg" for nine months, had operations on my eyes, and speech therapy, and was no longer able to live at home, so they sent me to Melbourne. I had to learn how to walk and talk again, and had to do some more education. It was really frustrating, particularly because of my cognitive problems.'

By 2004 Jeff was back on track, a little the worse for wear

but with some certificates in management: front line, disability and computer database. He was set up to do something with his life.

'I went looking for the children from my second marriage and found them through the police. At first my ex wouldn't let me see them; in effect, she had discriminated against my disability'. By this time Jeff was under the auspices of the Brotherhood of St Laurence, with Joe Spano as his contact worker. They had been helping with services such as housework and shopping, so that Jeff could get on with his pursuits. 'It was a godsend, as it allowed me to get back to normality.

'I took my wife to court to regain the right to see my children, who were now ten and twelve. They had counselling to prepare them to reconnect. I agonised over this, for their sake: was it all worth it? The date was set to meet them. It was a very emotional moment. My daughter threw her arms around me, and said "Thank God you are alive! I only remember someone who loved me." And the judge ruled for continued and open visitation rights – access every second weekend and turn about on holidays.

'My drive to give back to the community came from this moment. I work as a volunteer with Straight Arrows, a peer-support group, and talk to groups, particularly young people, about HIV-related issues and safe behaviour. In 2006 I was nominated to take the baton for the relay for the Commonwealth Games, and also received awards for my educational achievements. My children came from Perth and the whole family got together. Then in 2007 a certificate arrived from the National Australia Day Council, congratulating me on being nominated for the Australian of the Year Award 2008.

'The Brotherhood has helped me through all of this, giving me a better quality of life than I have ever had, even assistance in buying a car to maintain my independence. I have gone from being dependent and depressed to living a full life and one of a much higher standard than before. I'm free to get on with educating young people and working to make a difference to other people's lives, and I am grateful for this. Making a difference, and encouraging young people to be safe, are rewarding.'

Jonny O'Connor

'I saved a sparrow today . . .' Jonny O'Connor knows that he is a participant in the world who can make his own way and in so doing make a difference to others. When you walk into his space, you are faced with what seem to be a whole lot of contradictions. He was a professional boxer, and he looks like one too; he's a big rough guy. On the day we meet he has saved a tiny sparrow and this reminded him that God has given him a real sense of accomplishment, wants him to be gentle and mindful of a bigger picture.

Jonny has an intuition about people and their needs that is heartfelt and giving. He has generously prepared a platter which, he laughingly tells me, is called antipasto; I am not sure whether he is amused by the sophisticated title of the dish, or the fact that he has found himself creating food like this – it would have been unthinkable once. He has learnt to be a chef, and there are some serious cookbooks and kitchen equipment in his room, and the presentation of the platter is impressive. There is a friend, Harry, with him; they attend AA meetings together, and he is someone for

whom Jonny has cared for many years. Harry is quiet, but you feel his deep and proud admiration for his 'mate', who is so generous in his hospitality, who provides a warm space to visit and wonderful companionship.

But Jonny, for all his 'out-there' confidence – and he is a self-confessed ladies' man – admits to loneliness and a need for solitude. Time alone gives him the opportunity to focus on himself and his relationship with the God he loves. 'My faith has helped me to stop thinking about myself. God reminds me to be kind and thoughtful.' There is something about the companionship he has found through the care and the community of the church which has encouraged him to engage in life and friendship.

In Jonny's home there is a large box full of memorabilia: newspaper interviews and books where he is mentioned for his sporting prowess as well as his connection to the Builders Labourers Federation in its heyday. He has had a long journey, going from fighting greats like Lester Ellis and Graeme Brook to losing his confidence through the breakdown of his relationship and ensuing estrangement from his children, in which alcohol played a big role. He is proud to show you these mementos from his successes in life, but he is also definite in accepting the pain of the past and getting on with the reality of today.

Jonny was born in Melbourne's Royal Women's Hospital in 1961; tiny, he nearly died at birth. He was the oldest of six children.

After the third child, his sister Sharon, was born there was a ten-year gap before the other three came along. Jonny realised at this point that he had become a father figure to his siblings at the age of sixteen. His Dad, Kevin, was unsupportive, negative and jealous of anyone doing better than him. Beverly, his mother, one of thirteen children herself, was lovely and loving.

When he was fifteen, Jonny had a brush with the law. 'I pinched a pack of smokes and got caught. The coppers asked me if there was anything I was good at. There was one thing, fighting; I was boxing as an amateur at fifteen.' He soon progressed to the professional arena.

As Jonny tells the stories, his friend nods in agreement. The tales are true and always have an underpinning concern for social justice, which both gives them bite and affords a window into his life – his view. He says he loves bible stories, stuff from the 'wisdom literature', the Jesus story. They help him make sense of his life, they have taught him about compassion and how to give.

Jonny had two children – a daughter and a son – and was happily settled in Reservoir, a suburb north of Melbourne. 'Things just went bad and our relationship broke down. I had access to the kids for a couple of years but then my partner got married – I was the old couch and he was the new couch.' At the age of 33, after a lot of the 'big' things happened, Jonny found himself unemployed and unmotivated. He was staying at a mate's house. 'I wasn't working and I didn't feel good about myself. I had nowhere to live; I wasn't fit. I had let myself go.' He went to seek help and found the Sacred Heart Mission and the Argyle Street Housing Service in St Kilda. It was the best move he ever made. Sacred Heart helped him get his life together and secure his own public housing flat. He gained the confidence to seek work and a new role in competition sport.

But for Jonny the most important transformation was that he developed the courage to have a life-changing reunion with his daughter, whom he had not seen in more than a decade. This gave him the chance to rebuild his relationship with her. 'One day she turned to me and said, "My mum was wrong about you." ' He feels good about this, and proud that he has children to show for his life.

There was a time when he lost everything. A builder's labourer, he wouldn't join the 'scab' workers during strikes, and from this also came a violent and aggressive time. These days, though, you feel that his home is a place of peace. There is a certain chaos and joyful eclecticism about the things he's collected – a second-hand vanity mirror that still has the price written across the glass, a couple of TVs. His 'gift' as he sees it, is his defence of others. He's learnt much about compassion from conversations with his friends at the mission – Sisters Rose and Assumption and Father Ernie Smith – the ones he trusts and loves.

For all Jonny's gusto and enthusiasm, he is sensitive and he feels wounded at times. This lack of confidence comes, he feels, from his father, from his negativity, nastiness and cruelty. The AA meetings have been important to Jonny, giving him a place where he can relate and talk to others and feel supported. His life as he sees it now is about conversation, reflection and thinking. He has special mentors and friends like Melbourne personalities Tommy Hafey, Stan Alves, Peter Cullen and Father Ernie, who from time to time have picked him up and given him a chance and the hope to move beyond the negativities of the past. 'You can't always put your finger on why people reach out to me and why I have such wonderful friendships, but it's all part of the mystery of faith, of God.' His friend nods; he has heard it a million times before, but is glad Jonny has told me.

'I saved a sparrow today, and remembered God's peace, His mystery.'

Father Ken
Hodgson

Ken lives at Keble Court in Brunswick and has a family connection with Father Gerard Kennedy Tucker, founder of the Brotherhood. Ken's mother was first cousin to Bishop Reginald Stephen (first of Newcastle and then of Tasmania), whose wife was Father Tucker's sister. Coincidentally, we have the bishop's own chair, from Tasmania, at the Brotherhood office in Fitzroy.

Ken was born in Gormanston (a town which no longer exists but which was about six kilometres from Queenstown) on the west coast of Tasmania in 1926. His father was a personnel officer for the Mt Lyell Mining and Railway Company, whose historic railway line between Queenstown and Regatta Point closed down in 1963; some of its carriages are now used on the Puffing Billy Railway in Melbourne's Dandenong Ranges. (The Mt Lyell railway has since been reconstructed, and reopened in 2002.) Apparently there were no roads into the settlement and it would take two days to get out of the town and reach Hobart; these days it's a four-hour drive.

While Ken was still very young the family moved to Queenstown, where he attended both the primary and junior technical high schools. The focus of the high school was to provide apprentices for the mines, but Ken's interests steered him to more intellectual inquiry and he says he received a very good education in the best, old-fashioned sense of the term. He even did shorthand typing, which was later useful to him.

From the age of nine Ken can clearly remember wanting to go into the Church; there was something about 'the doctrine of the resurrection' that intrigued and enticed him.

From the age of nine Ken can clearly remember wanting to go into the Church; there was something about 'the doctrine of the resurrection' that intrigued and enticed him. He had heard of the Brotherhood of St Laurence and what was then the Keble House theological school in Brunswick, where Father Tucker lived. The area was a fearful slum in those days and many of the now-gentrified houses had dirt floors.

The Brotherhood's Father Coaldrake went to Tasmania to meet Ken's parents and to convince them that Keble House would be a good place for Ken to study. He was finally allowed to go, aged seventeen. The strict, monastic, timetabled life which Tucker had prescribed was too tough – and, Ken reflects, a misguided notion of the religious way of life – so instead he went into residence at Melbourne University's Trinity College with a full scholarship and did an Honours BA in History and English. Father Tucker and Ken had a parting of the ways; Keble House was closed and later the present Keble Court flats were built, where Ken lives now.

Ken was ordained as a deacon in the Anglican Church in September 1949, in the diocese of St Arnaud. He saw happy times at places like Mildura, which was known as the 'sunset country' and 'soldier settlement' district. Later he went to London to study church history at King's College and to do a curacy at St Ciprian's, Clarence Gate (Charles Dickens country). He returned to Australia as an assistant at All Saints' Anglican Cathedral in Bathurst; he then came back to Melbourne, where he lived with an aunt before being received into the Catholic Church in 1957.

Ken was taken to meet Archbishop Mannix to seek support for his shift to the Catholic Church. His own family rejected him because of his 'changing over' – his sisters accused him of practising 'voodooism', such was the strength of their objections. Ken's godmother had died in 1956 and had left him 10 000 pounds, with which he took his mother around the world and visited many religious sites. He then went to Rome for four years to study for the Catholic priesthood – he was ordained there on 7 April 1962 at the Basilica of St John Lateran, Rome's Catholic Cathedral.

Back in Melbourne, Ken was invited by the Bishop of

Maitland to go to Newcastle to found a secondary college, which was for him a very happy experience. He was asked to return to Tasmania as administrator of the Cathedral, but instead went to Reading in England to become a teacher and chaplain at Presentation College, a boarding school. He also spent time at St Bede's, a De La Salle Brothers boarding school in the Melbourne suburb of Mentone; and he lived at St Joseph's seminary in Michigan, USA, for 23 years.

While in Michigan, Ken contracted bone cancer, which manifested itself in his leg, so he retired and came back to Australia for treatment, as this was too expensive in the US. The cancer is ongoing but in Melbourne he did 'supply' work for the Catholic Church, which would involve crazy weekends where he took Mass in Hampton, then flew to Adelaide for another Mass, after which he would drive to Mildura to continue the circuit.

As you walk into Ken's place you find an altar permanently set with chalice and paten, burse and veil, in preparation for the Holy Mysteries.

Despite their unresolved estrangement, Father Tucker had always promised Ken that if he needed somewhere to live there would always be a place for him. So when Ken retired from active ministry in 1998 he went to live at Keble Court, moving to Carrum Downs in 2005 but returning to Keble in 2008. As you walk into Ken's place you find an altar permanently set with chalice and paten, burse and veil, in preparation for the Holy Mysteries. He proudly tells me that Archbishop Hart has licensed him to say Mass and to hear confessions at home.

His experience of moving from the Anglican tradition to Catholicism has, Ken believes, broadened his mind. He calls himself a Catholic ecumenist, the result of a long spiritual journey which, he admits, has 'not been all beer and skittles' and along which path he has been very sorely tested. Yet for Ken, the Brotherhood of St Laurence has always been his touchstone and it has continued to draw him back. He remembers with fondness being Father Tucker's secretary in his little office in Royal Arcade in the city while Ken was a student at Keble House. Downstairs, below the office, he would often help out in the shop when there was a shortage of staff. He helped Father Tucker type all the speeches for appeals and radio conversations, and he remembers the long line of influential people, particularly G. J. Coles, who would drop in for a chat and to support their old friend. As Tucker was dying, he was so respected in the community that the hospital wouldn't take a penny for his care. While Tucker was hard on those who left the fellowship of the Brotherhood as he had established it, Ken saw that he recognised the bigger picture – that the Brotherhood and its purpose had precedence in the greater scheme of things.

Ken's many papers and journals and books and religious objects have gathered dust. Yet he remains faithful not only as one of God's priests but also to Father Tucker who, though tough and uncompromising, built a place to which many like Ken could come home at the end of their long journey.

Kevin
Dangerfield

Sometimes it is difficult to know where the truth lies. A story is a story is a story, and some are more fantastic than others. Some tales are the weaving together of many lives, both real and imaginary; the timelines don't always quite match with history as we know it and a life story may even take us to fictional places.

Occasionally I come across a character whose displacement in life is so acute that their story speaks of a deep longing for connection and acceptance. It is an anchor which allows that person to say, 'This is where I am from, and this is the world I know; here I am safe. And if anybody asks, my story will be as complex and as rich as the next.'

Kevin is a kind and simple guy who has built a world around himself that gives him a framework within which to engage. He has chosen particular communities and groups and places where he can be safe, connected, valued and, above all, accepted. His life story is carefully constructed and, while it does contradict some of the facts we know, it contains moments of truth that help me understand his need to be constantly on the move. This is Kevin's story as he tells it.

Kevin was born on 9 December 1950. He says he was born in England in a town called Aidensfield and is quick to point out that 'That's where the TV show *Heartbeat* was filmed.' He spent his early childhood there and travelled, he says, to 'Midsomer', where that other famous television series is set, to attend school.

At the age of five or six, 'during the Second World War', Kevin, along with other children, was removed from his parents for 'national security' reasons and sent to Australia to be fostered out or adopted. 'The journey was long because we were "waylaid" in Brazil, as the Americans requisitioned the ship for naval purposes, and we had to wait a month for another ship. Later we were delayed in Java for six weeks, as the Dutch replacement ship had engine problems. Finally we arrived in Fremantle, and the people who were meant to take me and some of the other kids just didn't turn up! After several days at the shipping terminal, all us children were put on a train to Melbourne, where they sent us to an orphanage in Clarendon Street in South Melbourne. I was only six years old when I went there and I was there for most of the time until I was 22, except for some short stays with foster families.'

The family stays didn't last for very long and Kevin says they were pretty rough. 'How would you feel at the age of six having to chop firewood all day with an axe you couldn't lift, or to carry a bag of wheat or a bale of hay? How would you like to be called useless and verbally abused by your hosts just because you were too young and too weak to do what they wanted you to do? Every time, it would not work out and they would send me back to the orphanage.'

After a while the children were moved from the big orphanage into smaller premises around the corner in Cecil Street. To Kevin his childhood was marked by constantly being on the move and he feels that this has kept him, and others like him, restless. He tells me of a friend called Philip, his companion in all this.

> To Kevin his childhood was marked by constantly being on the move and he feels that this has kept him, and others like him, restless.

'In the meantime, there was no schooling, just manual work. That's all we did, so I wasn't learning anything. And my friend Philip, who was born in Melbourne but lived in the orphanage too, was in the same boat. He never knew why he was there, and wouldn't talk about it anyway. Some things happened, and I won't talk about that either, but they happened to the both of us all the time.'

Kevin says he finally left the orphanage when it was sold. 'A council lady took us to Social Security to find us a place to live, to have us registered and to organise a pension . . . In those days it was pounds, shillings and pence. Philip went off by himself and I have no idea where he is to this day.'

For years Kevin travelled from town to town, to the places where he could find menial work – places like Geelong, Laverton, Melton, Cobram, Shepparton and Alexandra, where he remembers having the longest stay. He worked as a shearer and as a cabinet-maker's apprentice, cutting out doors and holes for kitchen sinks. He lived on farms and slept outdoors, often just relying on his swag. Finally he returned to Melbourne and gained employment at a firm in North Melbourne, which made billiard tables and coffins. He found a room in a boarding house in nearby Queensberry Street.

'I came to work one morning, and the cleaners had failed to put salt and sawdust on the floor to cover the grease. I had a bad fall, with several breaks and fractures, including my skull. I had to be dismissed and they were only going to pay me for 33 days! I found some lawyers in South Melbourne – two ladies who took up the case and won. I got a payout and the money is still in the bank; it's keeping me for the rest of my life.

'After my accident I was stuck in my room looking at four walls, and I became restless. I found a country newspaper and they were looking for workers, so off I went shearing again. I told my employers that I suffered from occasional back pain and they said they could teach me wool-classing. I stayed for some time and liked being there.'

Kevin returned again to Melbourne and settled first in Kensington, then in Hanover Street, North Melbourne, where he lives today. He says he is on the pension and has tried to do some study and schooling, though has no head for mathematics. He likes to write and has a dream to do the VCE; he'd even like to do a Masters. But he says that his accident caused some brain damage, and he has problems remembering things and being able to follow things through. 'Part of me responds to a request or challenge, but then I can't

'I found the Brotherhood and the Coolibah Centre through my case worker. I find this place very supportive; it has done a lot for me.'

make it work in my head. I have done some volunteer work, but I find it difficult to work with others and to respond when they ask me to do things. It's hard for me to keep up with the pace.

'I found the Brotherhood and the Coolibah Centre through my case worker, who brought me here and introduced me to the manager. It's close to where I live, and I find this place very supportive; it has done a lot for me. I need time and patience to deliver, because of my head trauma from the work accident, and Marica and Rod and the others are very supportive. I've had a rough life.'

In early 2007, we celebrated the marriage of a couple who had met at the Coolibah, and Kevin was one of the guests. At the end of the ceremony, he approached me and asked if I did baptisms as well. He had always wanted to be baptised so his name would be recognised by St Peter, who Kevin had adopted as his saint! We spent several weeks in conversation, reading through the order of service for baptism, and studying scripture to help him understand the meaning and origin of the ritual. Eventually a date was set and many people, including staff and members of Coolibah, came to witness this special moment. Kevin expressed all the delight and joy that might be seen in a child's face at a significant moment in life. We named him, and blessed him as we poured water over his forehead, and people embraced and rejoiced with him.

Giving Kevin this opportunity helped to tell his story, his truth. I was struck with another truth as I listened to him – that if as a child he was denied schooling and was sent out to do menial work instead, we as a society had failed him, in that an education is a fundamental right of every human being. His social, emotional and cognitive skills were not developed as they should have been.

Who knows what the deeper truth of Kevin's life is. He is an articulate person who desires to be included in the dance of life. He always presents as well as he can, and with dignity. His ability to reflect on issues, or on faith and scripture, is often surprising; he is able to think and analyse, to connect to the problems of the bigger world, while at the same time becoming quickly lost in his own. It is critically important that we offer him a place where he may be safe. He has mapped his course through some scary territory and he has landed safely, even though there have been some adventures along the way.

Maureen
O'Connor

Maureen O'Connor, a member of the Brotherhood's Coolibah Centre in Fitzroy, is Jonny O'Connor's aunt (Jonny also features in this book). She has recently joined the Choir of Hard Knocks and this has added a positive dimension to her life.

Recently the choir attended a function at Government House, where Maureen had the unexpected honour of meeting the Governor's wife, Mrs De Kretser. In conversation, Mrs De Kretser asked Maureen whether she'd been to Government House before. Maureen replied, 'No, I haven't. It's so beautiful and big, it would make the ideal place for homeless people, because there are so many of them living on the streets and this place is so big!' Mrs de Kretser thanked Maureen for her comments and moved on. 'Well, Father Jeff,' says Maureen, 'there's no point in beating about the bush!'

There is an innocent kindness and bluntness about Maureen. She likes to laugh and she laughs easily; she tells you when something's up, or when something really nice has happened. She shares the concerns of the world and of her family and friends, and communicates that without hesitation. She is trusting. She comes to chapel, but leaves at 'The Peace' because she is a Catholic and it's an Anglican service. She's been taught that and it won't be undone!

Maureen and I have a joke that stems from a silly moment before a choir performance one afternoon in spring. She was wearing a very colourful floral skirt, and asked me what I thought she looked like. I replied, 'Well, a bowl of fruit salad, of course', at which she laughed. Ever since, no matter what she is wearing, we play the game and her response is always the same: 'You cheeky bugger.' Then we get on with the day. She reports what she sees and how she feels, and while there is often a lot of repeated information when people engage in conversation with her at the Coolibah, you realise the intrinsic point she is making is justice for all. For this reason she is a surprising woman, uncomplicated yet with a deep integrity that belies her tough journey. Why shouldn't Government House become a shelter for the homeless – they are, after all, citizens of Victoria and as deserving of such a beautiful space as any other citizen!

Maureen was orphaned at an early age, and she can vaguely remember her parents' funerals taking place in Melbourne's General Cemetery. She was only a child, but the vision of those days is firmly implanted in her memory: they were Public Trustee funerals – 'paupers' services' – and there was little marking of the graves. Over the years Maureen became deeply troubled about this, and felt that, no matter how poor her parents had been or even how poor she might be, they deserved the recognition that everyone is entitled to. She embarked on the challenging quest, with scant resources, to find exactly where her parents were buried and to organise appropriate commemorative plaques, for their sake and for her own. She believed that until the plaques were installed her parents effectively remained homeless, that she had to restore to them some dignity and peace.

Maureen has involved herself in the Unsung Hero's program at the Coolibah, which was developed by the Brotherhood in conjunction with Melbourne Grammar School, one of the city's oldest and most prestigious schools. Through this program, a member of Coolibah pairs up with a Year 10 student who is seeking to understand, and document, the life journey of a person living in poverty – it is an eye-opening exercise for many of these affluent lads. Maureen's partner, Jordan, is taking the experience very seriously and has been deeply attentive to Maureen and her story. Finding the graves of her parents became an irresistible challenge for him, and he threw himself into the search with Maureen. They walked their feet off, made many inquiries and finally pinpointed the spot. Maureen stood and looked, and wept. This was the place where she remembered standing as a young girl at her parents' funerals, and it was an emotional moment: 'As though I had come home, Father Jeff, and found what I had been looking for.' This was also a moment of justice for her. 'Everyone deserves a home in life and in death, and the spot needs to be marked so people know who's there.' When she realised that the grave isn't far from the Prime Ministers' Memorial Garden, she was particularly chuffed.

Maureen took out a loan, and had brass plaques made for the graves, and when they were installed a few of us gathered for a service of dedication. She had covered the site in flowers, plastic and real, and photos and knick-knacks; it was once again a familial place. Her memories, her right to a marked place for her parents, had been recognised; justice had been found. Jordan was there, and Maureen had brought soft drink and Twisties and treats for us all to share. We stood in the pavilion of the Prime Minister's Garden, rain gently falling, and Maureen told us the story over and over again. She heaped attention on Jordan in gratitude for his attentiveness; he is her hero, and he deserves the very best.

Maureen has had a tough life. Her memories are connected to the addresses where she has lived, including the odd rooming-house, to a life of little security. There have been moments of abuse; she doesn't want to talk about those things, but she does want to tell the truth about herself, because the truth matters. She has had wonderful times, and real happiness too, has a keen sense of justice and looks out for those she loves.

Maureen started her life in Melbourne in Richmond, and was born in a private hospital in Highett Street to Ellen and William O'Connor. The elder of two children, she had a brother called Kevin. The family lived on Rowena Parade in Richmond and she had a typical inner-city childhood, playing in the streets and lanes, getting up to some tomboy stuff and plenty of mischief. There wasn't much money and by Grade 5 she had left school and got a job with a bookbinder, gluing the spines of books. Her mother had a series of strokes, after the last of which she never came out of hospital; and her father died 'of the drink', and she doesn't much want to talk about that. Maureen got together with a guy called 'Blackjack', and she doesn't want to talk about him much either, but in the end she found some happiness with a man called Merv Parker and they had three daughters together. But because of the hard times they lived in, the family went from Commission houses and flats to boarding houses and the children were taken from her and fostered out.

Maureen now has seven grandchildren and several great-grandchildren, some of whom have been in foster care too. One great-grandchild was born with severe medical conditions and within hours of being born was operated on at the Royal Children's Hospital. We didn't see Maureen for weeks at that time, for the whole of her focus was on being as near as she could be to her great-grandchild. But her networks are good and we heard plenty of reports of her progress from her mates; it was touch-and-go for a while. Finally she reappeared and was happy and reflective, but you could see that it had taken an emotional toll on her. 'This is what life is like for people like us,' she says. 'We have to live with that and be grateful for what we have.'

Maureen is one of the bright lights of the Coolibah – she is colourful, argumentative, and full of news and hope. She has formed a deep, mother-like attachment to her nephew Jonny; we hear of his exploits and his ringing her up at 3 a.m., but she doesn't mind because she loves him so much and has always been there for him. Jonny does come into the Coolibah occasionally, but we know most about him through her stories. She and I still joke about what she's wearing, but we know when to be serious and she'll establish those terms as the encounter begins. We respect her for that.

> 'This is what life is like for people like us. We have to live with that and be grateful for what we have.'

Mr and Mrs Hu

We now have the benefit of knowing something of the stories of the people of China in the twentieth century, which were for a long time largely covered up by the communist régime. Mr and Mrs Hu, children of Shanghai in the 1930s, were both from large families. Their childhoods were marked by cruelty at the hands of the Japanese during their occupation of the city from 1937, and by the ensuing corrupt Chinese government, which for a moment had seemed to promise liberation.

Mr Hu lived, with his five brothers and a sister, in a house opposite Shanghai's French Quarter and he remembers well the French children coming and going to school. In the same district was the very visible Japanese army base, with its wire fences and its sentries on all corners displaying shining bayonets.

'Japanese soldiers were very bad men: to them, killing people was like a normal daily activity. But by 1945 we entered into a happy time when the Japanese emperor surrendered. In primary school we were forced to study Japanese, but we didn't like it and would mock the language by changing the meanings; it was fun.

We didn't like our life under them; we had to eat mouldy rice, as they used to take all the good food. After the Japanese occupation we thought life would be better and more stable, but the civil war between the nationalists and the communists began soon afterwards and for many years it was a very unhappy time. In 1948–9, the communists came into power, which brought some stability.

'While I was a middle-school student my oldest brother joined the campaign against the war between the nationalists and the communists. He took part in a demonstration to protest against the government doing things many people saw as oppressive. There were government spies in Shanghai at the time, looking for anyone who might be suspicious – and they took my brother away. They cleverly used him in their anti-communist propaganda by making him talk about how the communists made children spy on and work against their parents. Our parents were forced to testify that he was a good son. My brother had become well known in Shanghai, so he had to be released; he became a spy for the government in many places, but they had him dismissed as a university student and closely watched by spies in Shanghai. Finally he fled and went north of the Yangtze River to the district occupied by the communists – he joined the very people the government was fighting. Sadly, he contracted meningitis, and he died in the city of Yangzhou.

'I and other members of the family were, of course, affected by all these events. I was dismissed from my school, which my father thought was because my work was poor but that was not true. I was sent to another middle school, where I worked very hard and became the Number One student. On 25 May 1949, Shanghai was liberated by the communists. It was a time of rejoicing – a very joyful period, almost like when the Japanese had surrendered. We finally felt there was some hope for us. After the liberation I re-entered my old school and passed all my exams. It was the best school in Shanghai.

'I met Mrs Hu at the electricity plant; she was my "boss". It was love at first sight; I was captivated by her.'

'Because I was well educated the communists asked me to work for the government. After graduation I worked during the day in an electricity plant and studied engineering at night. I became an engineer and worked for a period, then became a senior engineer, but there was not much joy as by this time I was already over 50 years of age. This period in China was full of meetings, study and discussion – no time to rest, always fighting with each other. I worked right up until I retired at the age of 60 (in China the rule is that men retire at sixty and women at 55).

'I met Mrs Hu at the electricity plant; she was my "boss". It was love at first sight; I was captivated by her. My parents insisted that I become financially independent before I could get married, that I make and save enough money to support a family. I honoured their point of view. Eventually, on 1 October 1955, which is China's National Day, we got married; now we have been married for 53 years and are still very happy. We have two children, a boy who lives in Canada and a girl who lives in Brisbane. In 2006 I went back to China to see my son before he moved to Canada. My daughter came to Melbourne in 1991 to join her husband, and in 2006 they moved to Brisbane.'

Mrs Hu, the 'leader' of his household, came to Australia in 1996. She gained residency and was able to bring her husband across in 2000; he had to apply three times. They lived in Coburg and Mr Hu's first impression of Australia was that it was very hot. Their tin-roofed house was west-facing, and very hot at night. Leaving China was difficult for Mr Hu, but he came because 'the boss' had decided this would be a really good place to live – and she has no desire to go back to China.

Mr Hu has been a very keen pool player for many years and a few years ago he discovered the Brotherhood's Coolibah Centre. He thought it was a wonderful place and, while he doesn't play as much pool as he used to, he has found the fellowship and companionship of the Coolibah members very enriching. It's a two-way exchange, as Mr Hu has been an invaluable resource in helping to translate and mediate for other Chinese members. He is philosophical about leaving China and quotes an old Chinese saying:

'China is my birthplace and I miss it a lot. My dreams at night are always of China, but this is also human nature and not so unusual for as we get older we always go back and dream of our youth.'

'Falling leaves always go back to their roots'.

'China is my birthplace and I miss it a lot. My dreams at night are always of China, but this is also human nature and not so unusual for as we get older we always go back and dream of our youth. As my "boss" says, Australia is a very good place with clean air and good water. I feel the Australian government and people are good and friendly, and the Coolibah is a very good place to be. Sometimes when people leave after a short time I am very sad because I don't want them to leave. Ann, our Coolibah worker, is going; I'm grateful to her, and I wish she wasn't leaving.'

You see Mr Hu helping to set up for lunch in the Coolibah dining room, conversing with other members, as is Mrs Hu; he is keenly called to the pool room for a game. Mr Hu greets everyone with a smile and a bow of the head; the couple are gentle and very concerned for the people who come through our doors. They share a good rapport with the staff, who feel comfortable asking their advice about the many Chinese people who are now finding their way into the Coolibah. Many of them live in the high-rise flats of Fitzroy, Collingwood and Richmond, and each morning they gather to share breakfast and conversation as they begin their day. You see some of the very elderly doing their daily ritual of tai chi, respectful of the place they've found and of sharing in the lives of others.

Peter Griffin

Peter is one of those guys you look at and wonder about his life – has he done anything, been anywhere – and you could be forgiven for thinking that there is a certain sadness, a possibility that his has been a journey of missed opportunities. He is keen to connect and to be of help, and his peers sometimes criticise him for this. Maybe they see him as being too frail to carry through his offer. He is gentle, thoughtful, mindful of the community he spends his days in, and for that reason there is something very reassuring about his presence both at the Coolibah Centre and in Millot House, where he lives with others he cares for very much.

Peter is tallish and gangly, a little stooped, and when he wears shorts you realise his legs are like pins, belying his younger days of serious rugby playing. He's part of the family – not a philosopher, or even a storyteller, but he will laugh at the moment, and there is the keen look of an observer in his eyes, which invites social commentary in spontaneous conversation. It makes you glad to see him.

Peter Griffin was born in Wollongong on 27 June 1957. As a teenager his great love was for rugby league, which he played until he was 20. Home was near the sea, and while he was still at school he could be found on the beach every afternoon when school was finished for the day. Times were good; life was good, he had plenty of friends. He was even invited to play rugby on a tour to England and France as part of an Australian schoolboys team, but he broke an arm and the loss of that opportunity shattered him.

When Peter was sixteen his father died, and with a mother and siblings to support he had to leave school. The family were fortunate because they owned their house, but Peter was forced to move swiftly into the bread-winner role. Leaving school to go to work was a simple fact; it was his duty to look after his family. After some years Peter got a job at Port Kembla working with BHP. He would always send money home when he had work, which was often as there were plenty of opportunities in the early 1970s and it was easy to get casual jobs. He moved all around the country.

In 1979 came an incredible opportunity for a new venture. A group of friends had put together a band called Taquin, and Peter was invited to become part of the support crew – a roadie. He loved this life: it gave him freedom, connectedness, a sense of community with the band and crew, and seemed to link to his gift for helping people achieve their dreams. Ten years in the music industry made him a highly sought-after expert in his field; Cold Chisel was the first big group he toured with. He worked hard, often day and night without breaks, and while being on the road was a great experience, its craziness was exhausting and unrelenting. The list of groups and musicians Peter has worked with is impressive: Rose Tattoo, Heaven, AC/DC, Dire Straits, Icehouse, Del Shannon, Tina Turner, and many more. He could be relied on to do the job quickly, efficiently and on the run.

'On one trip, while I was working with Tina Turner, we had to drive from Darwin to Adelaide. When we got to the border we were told not to go through as the roads were flooded and dangerous because they were still unmade in those days. We kept going, and about a hundred miles or so down the road we rolled the truck. People were hurt and it was a couple of hours before someone came along, some locals. We saw the lights coming towards us; they were on the way back to their station. They took us to Coober Pedy Hospital, and later we were transferred to Adelaide Hospital. It was a scary business, but we were alright.'

Part of the nature of the work and its culture was drugs: 'All around you. Never took a needle; took speed, but not with a needle'. One of the toughest gigs was with Del Shannon: 'Six weeks with only two roadies, so we existed on speed . . . Cairns one day, Melbourne the next. We never took speed recreationally, but just to stay awake at night so you could do your job, so you could get from A to B in time for the next show.

'Getting to know the bands and the people around them was great. Because you were visiting the same venues over and over, with different bands, you'd get to know the people who lived in those communities. You became good friends and would catch up with them on your return visits.'

'We never took speed recreationally, but just to stay awake at night so you could do your job, so you could get from A to B in time for the next show.'

Despite the drugs keeping him going, by the time he was in his thirties Peter had become too old and was no longer useful to the industry. He was a physical wreck and could not keep up the pace. The next six years saw him back in 'mainstream' work until a serious back injury as the result of a forklift accident ended his career. Unable to work and on a pension, Peter arrived in Melbourne for medical treatment. He liked the city and has found a home and sense of community here. The Coolibah Centre is a place where he feels he can make a contribution. He is captain of the Coolibah pool team, and is a volunteer with the St Vincent de Paul soup van, which delivers meals to those in need. Fridays are of particular interest, because young volunteers come from regional centres like Lilydale, Bendigo, Ballarat and Horsham to help to distribute food to people in the boarding houses, and Peter has taken up a mentoring role, going to the rooms with the volunteers to make sure everything is safe for them.

He also gets out and about. 'I go down to the Fitzroy Pool for the day occasionally and do some exercise in the water. It feels good after I have done it, and I like going to the gym class they have there too. They have lots of good people there, and I enjoy meeting them. I still go to the beach now and then, but I like to stay home at night.'

All he has gone through has taken a toll on Peter's health. His calcium count and his medications have to be continually monitored, and he has monthly blood tests, resulting in occasional stays in hospital, which he

'I've got to 50 and this has made me so happy. And I'll live a little longer. I'm thankful.'

doesn't like because it means taking up precious beds. He also suffers from asthma. Peter has two daughters, by different mothers. One is at uni in Brisbane and the youngest is a child-care worker in Wollongong. Peter enjoys good contact with them as well as with his mum. They always ring him, so it doesn't cost him too much to keep in touch. He sees his mum about once a year and catches up with the girls at least two or three times a year.

Peter will tell you that he has had a good life, that he is

easygoing and never violent. There are no drugs in his life now, although he likes a couple of drinks at night. He is thoughtful about the needs of others, and keeps his eye out for his neighbours, particularly his 97-year-old next-door neighbour. He is a person of hope, which is bound up in his desire for relationship and community.

'I've got to 50 and this has made me so happy. And I'll live a little longer. I'm thankful.'

Rhonda Hamley

I first met Rhonda 20 years ago, when I was a theological student doing a placement at the Brotherhood. She was dressed in what I would describe as a 'chemist's/nursing assistant's uniform': blue, practical, and essential to what she was doing at the time – caring for two men named Frankie and Michael. Rhonda was a formidable woman, terrifying to the greenhorn I was then, with her flame-red hair loosely pulled up into a bun and a defiant look on her face. Her stunningly blue eyes seemed to be searching for any potential injustice and she was quick to comment, which backed up my feeling of, 'Oh, my God, I hope she doesn't notice me or, worse still, speak to me!' I was on her turf and I felt the pressure of my intrusion!

These days she is a little softer, a cardigan added to her 'uniform', her expression a little more reflective. But she is still passionate, and an edgy barometer of social justice. With the years her observations have become more intense and she sees the world of the inner city as one of extraordinary tension: on the one hand are the continued needs of the marginalised people she cares for, who are still filling the streets; on the other, the freshly painted, 'restored'

houses of Fitzroy and Collingwood could tell a million stories of the old (and, she would argue, 'real') community she knows and loves.

Rhonda is a great believer in democracy, as a forum via which to be heard. She is highly emotional and passionate, to the point of being accused of aggression, these characteristics being balanced by a strong sense of justice. The national flag is important to her, as are the British royal family and, particularly, the former Governor-General, her great friend and supporter Peter Hollingworth.

Rhonda was born Ronald Barry Hamley on 17 September 1941, at the Royal Women's Hospital. The second child of three (with sisters Yvonne and Judith), Rhonda knew from the very beginning, from the inside out, of the woman trapped in her male form. She struggled with this for the whole of her young life. When she dressed as a woman, her Irish father would make his feelings clear: 'A man should be a man.' She tried to repress her feelings, fought openly about it, was angry. When she had a sex-change operation in her 20s, she kept the essence of her birth name, as a symbol of her respect for her decision.

The journey was tough and painful, but Rhonda has ever remained loyal to those whose help, companionship and support she found along the way. Father Gerard Tucker opened the 'Green Door' (the door to the Brotherhood's drop-in centre and to the world of the Brotherhood), to Rhonda one Christmas when she was looking for a place to be safe in, to belong to. He was kind to her and, while she was too young to be a member of the Coolibah Centre, she was referred to the young chaplain, the Reverend Peter Hollingworth, who offered her support and pastoral care.

This was the beginning of her relationship with the Brotherhood, providing a stage on which she could grapple with and be supported in her difficulties. Many personal and soul-searching assessments, as well as psychological evaluations, were needed for her progression to womanhood. The wider family of the Brotherhood became listeners and reflectors in her journey – Mrs Sumner and her dog, Jessie Millot, Mrs Skinner, Sister Lyn Bathhurst and Marilyn Roper to name but a few – legendary characters and now namesakes of some of the Brotherhood's buildings. Rhonda knew and loved them all, as they loved her.

The night before her operation, emotionally exhausted by all that had gone before and all that lay ahead, Rhonda found her way to St Paul's Cathedral. She was questioning in her own mind whether going ahead with the change of gender was the right or wrong thing to do, because it flew in the face of what people in the community (people of all faiths) believed was right. There Archbishop Frank Woods found her and, sensing her turmoil, sat with her and listened; afterwards he took her to the altar and offered prayers with her and for her, and gave her a blessing for the days ahead. The compassion of the Church for Rhonda – from Gerard

Tucker and Peter Hollingworth to Archbishop Woods – was a testimony to the 'Christ-likeness' of its ministry, which people seldom know of. Rhonda still tells the story with deep emotion and gratitude.

That night Rhonda came to the realisation that after tomorrow there would be no need to suppress her feelings, or any opportunity to reflect on her decision. She had borne the pain and the weight of doubt, and the judgements of other people, for many years. Now she would be able to take responsibility for her own being, her own life. Because after all the assessments, and the advice and opinions of others, Rhonda realised in the end she had to make the decision for herself. It was her choice. The operation, which took place in the old Queen Victoria Hospital, lasted four hours; Rhonda remained in hospital for a month.

'At the end of the day, after the fight is fought and the anger is rendered, it's what lies in the heart that matters.'

Rhonda developed a passion for public speaking and social justice, variously visiting the Communist Party, the Democrats and the Liberal and Labor parties, to seek clarification of their direction and to act as a watchdog for the underdog! She wouldn't let them get away with anything, and often called them on an issue or a throwaway line; if it was going to be detrimental and deny people the right to speak in a democratic country, it had to be dealt with. She cut a formidable figure, and had a sharp and articulate tongue which most leaders of such bodies cowered from. It was not unheard of for Rhonda to be forcibly removed from meetings because of her resolve to deal with the issue then and there.

Her life had become a symphony of politics and personal struggle. Her personal story informed all her pursuits as an activist; it also tied in with her emotional struggle, her search for reassurance. Does God forgive? What will happen to me when I die? Why do people die? Rhonda's focus for her passion in all this, because of her experiences, is her belief that the centrality of the Church must be the care and support of people. She has discovered this through the care and modelling of Father Tucker and Father Peter Hollingworth. 'At the end of the day, after the fight is fought and the anger is rendered, it's what lies in the heart that matters. And I know what lies in mine: it is about care for others, and people's needs and rights, and I'm not about to let one person walk all over another just because they think they don't matter. People can be cruel, but it's usually out of ignorance'.

Rhonda's caring for others is impressive. There was Frankie, the blind man, who was completely alone and was able to depend on her for all his needs. Under medical supervision, she looked after him, fed him, washed him, and took him where he needed to go; she gave him the dignity necessary for him to live as part of a community. And later she also cared for Michael, who was Maltese and came from a broken home. He would come and help with Frankie, as his eyesight failed. Rhonda cared for them both honestly and generously, arranging for them to go on holidays and attend other activities. Michael died first, from a heart attack, followed by Frankie.

Years later, long after Frankie's death, the local policemen at Atherton Gardens still talk about the support they receive from her in their work, particularly with the young refugees. But that's Rhonda – she is always concerned for others and their safety. And she's not afraid to question and challenge the justice system and those in authority (always with respect, she's quick to add).

Yes, her care is an extension of her own need, but the harnessing of passion and anger, justice and love are expressed in her day-to-day activities. Those around her respect her space, and those who challenge her come out the other end with a greater understanding of who they are dealing with.

Rhonda sits in the Coolibah dining room on many afternoons, keenly observing the goings-on. Reminiscing, correcting, being a presence. We know she is there, and with all that has gone before, we acknowledge this story as a link to our own story too.

She says: 'I wish whoever reads this book to understand that this is what it means to be an Anglican – it's about truth, caring and understanding. A lot of people have their own views about what being an Anglican is all about – but this is what I believe. When I was a child the Anglican church was called the Church of England. Elderly people from the Brotherhood of St Laurence, who are no longer here with us, were caring, understanding and compassionate. The late Father Tucker, who founded the Brotherhood of St Laurence, came as a humble priest from Newcastle, and he came with a dream – and now his teachings are known all over Australia. I am proud to be associated with him and the Brotherhood of St Laurence and everything it represents. God bless.'

Roy Barrett

The story of the Hobbit comes to mind when I think of Roy, who is, quite literally, the gatekeeper of the car park of the Brotherhood's headquarters in Fitzroy. His little flat sits right by the gate and you will see him at all times of the day, sometimes with a bottle of Coca Cola in his hand, sometimes plaiting a huge ball of wool (which has grown over many years to twice the size of a basketball) sometimes checking the rubbish bins, which are all in tip-top order. He wanders up and down the car park, and is also in the Coolibah Centre for breakfast and lunch and at many other times. He can often be found sitting in at the edge of some activity, seemingly listening. Often he nods knowingly, so much so that I wish he could tell us what he understands!

Roy has few communication skills and has been diagnosed with intellectual disability, hearing impairment, memory loss and other medical problems. He is illiterate, and signs his name 'Berrett'. He is very softly spoken and mostly very hard to understand; it is often necessary to ask him to repeat himself, and you learn to listen to him very closely. It is difficult to get a conversation going unless you mention the ball of wool of which he is so proud, or his

extraordinary efforts as a marathon runner who has competed in more fun runs and marathons than we can count. He enters them all and as recently as 2008, at the age of 75, he did the annual Frankston–Melbourne run; he has been awarded many medals.

We know little about Roy other than that he was born in Geelong West in 1932, and that when he was about fourteen his parents died and he came to Melbourne; at that time he lost contact with his brothers and sisters. For many years he has resided in the Brotherhood's independent living units, and he attends the Coolibah Centre on a daily basis. He gets out and about, mostly in Brunswick Street. He is cared for by the Brotherhood, Southern Cross Care and the State Trustees. The support he receives is a wonderful example of how the most needy can be gathered up and given a sense of community and friendship that helps them feel safe and included. There is no doubt that Roy feels this is his home and he enters into as much of the activity at the Coolibah as possible, from carpet bowls or trying to help in the garden to sitting in on the weekly communion service – sometimes receiving communion and at other times just wandering off.

There are many members of the community who keep a quiet eye out for Roy and the examples of care and patience are heartening. He has a regular seat in the dining room, where he sits with Bill and Graham and Elyse. People make sure that a meal is put in front of him and that he has all he needs; he mostly takes his own dishes to the serving hatch at the end of the meal. Sometimes he is aware of your presence and will raise a hand to acknowledge that he has seen you, while at other times he's lost in his own world, but it is important to make sure that you always acknowledge him as this seems to bring him back on track. He will admit, if you ask, that he has problems with his memory, but cannot elaborate on how long this has been the case.

We know Roy enjoys every opportunity to participate in the life of the community, and the greater outward demonstration of this is his running. He's disciplined in his training and most mornings gets up at dawn to run up to sixteen kilometres; you will often see him in a T-shirt, a pair of silk boxer shorts and runners pacing his way up Victoria Parade, Queens Parade, Brunswick Street or somewhere in that area. Occasionally he'll appear with all his medals to show his achievements, and when you mention running and marathons he throws both hands in the air and says, 'Many, many runs, many years, from the olden days.' When he mentions the past, he invariably refers to it as 'the olden days'.

Roy was for a time an assistant coach for the Princes Hill football team, and a volunteer charity worker – our records show that he has collected more than 20 000 dollars for various charities and has held down a full-time job as a painter. He mentions that he worked for a long time and that he's lived at the Brotherhood for 20 years. He played with a dart team in 'the olden days' and was good at it – he says he never missed the board and once got four bullseyes in one day. He uses his hands to illustrate his story.

Twenty years ago Roy was referred to Roytal, a sheltered workshop in Kew, and at the age of 55 he landed his first full-time job since his teens, as a painter. Along with the job, he found new friends, support and stimulation, and while the job only paid about 50 dollars a week (plus lunch), it brought him great happiness. In all his years of running, he has not had any injuries and he has always finished a run even if it means walking. His great dream is to finish, for his age group, in a good position – he falls back into the chair and says, patting his chest, 'I would be a happy boy, very happy.'

Roy likes living at the Brotherhood. He likes to stand outside and watch the world go by, knowing that he can retreat quickly back into his space. He is a good gatekeeper and his gentle presence is reassuring to all who pass by.

Tom Millington

Tom Millington is a lovely person. He is the same age as me, and a reminder that as indestructible as we think we are it only takes a moment for our life to change completely and forever. One day, at the age of 40, Tom went to buy some milk; there had been rain, and Tom slipped on the steps of his verandah and broke two ribs. As a result of complications from this injury, his life was never the same again.

There was nothing particularly remarkable about Tom's childhood, other perhaps than that he was born in New Guinea. His dad worked for Ansett Airlines and his mum was a nurse; his sister was born in New Guinea too. He remembers little about New Guinea, as his parents separated when he was very young and his mother came to live with his grandparents on their farm in Colac, Victoria.

Later Tom's mother remarried and they moved to Karingal near Frankston, where he attended Ballam Secondary College. Sports have always been a great passion for Tom and his stepdad encouraged him to connect with soccer. After school he gained an apprenticeship with Nylex, and later on he worked as a technician with a lift company.

Tom tells me about Alyson, his wife, and their two sons, Gavin and Jaryd. He and Alyson are divorced now (which happened well before the accident) and the boys live with their mother in Mt Martha. Gavin has just finished VCE, has got his driving licence and is hoping to do an animation course; Jaryd is playing in the Mt Martha Seconds cricket team. At the moment Tom is not seeing the boys so much, as they are at an age where they are getting on with their own lives and activities.

> . . . Tom has extraordinary patience and resilience, seemingly awaiting an opportunity to connect and do something that will lead him beyond the moment and his disability.

When he had his fall, Tom had terrible problems with his breathing and a lot of pain. The doctor kept prescribing pain-killers but there were days when he couldn't get out of bed. One weekend, when his son was visiting, things were so bad he called an ambulance; it was discovered that Tom had major complications and a collapsed lung. Later they found that he had had a severe stroke, and there were further complications due to infection. Tom embarked on the long process of rehabilitation, living with a badly affected left side as well as suffering nausea and illness as a result of the many antibiotics he had to take. At this point in our conversation he admits that the stroke has affected his memory, so timelines are difficult for him. In talking to him, you understand that Tom has extraordinary patience and resilience, seemingly awaiting an opportunity to connect and do something that will lead him beyond the moment and his disability.

One day Tom noticed an advertisement for Adam's fitness class at the Brotherhood's Carrum Downs Tucker Village Settlement. Tom knew he'd come to the right place when he met Adam, who offered him a coffee the moment he arrived! Tom realised how unfit he was because of his condition, which became woefully obvious after he struggled but failed to lift a weight above his head while 80-year-old Elvie succeeded. He realised that this was going to be a challenge, and something he would enjoy doing. At the end of his first session, Adam gave Tom homework to help him get his legs stronger. He noticed that the woman next to him, Jodie, who suffers from the same condition as his, could do leg squats and lunge squats, and this provided the challenge he needed.

The experience was so positive and life-giving that Tom decided to do a personal training course. The repetition involved has been helpful for his memory problems. 'Adam does one-on-one classes and we have built up such a rapport that he gets me to take the class on Tuesdays. He coaches me through it, which means he sees me in action and can give me critical reflection and encouragement. Adam is a good teacher and has a great sense of humour. The stroke left me with no vision in one eye, and with the other stroke-related conditions this means that I have to find new or different ways of doing things, which can be very challenging.' Tom says that Adam thinks he is doing so well in his course that he will probably finish it early.

'The stroke left me with no vision in one eye, and with the other stroke-related conditions this means that I have to find new or different ways of doing things, which can be very challenging.'

Tom enjoys other activities as well, such as sailing and shooting, also under the auspices of the Brotherhood. He takes a certain pride in the fact that he lives in his own home, because his boys can come and spend time with him there. His mum brings good food and he is cheeky enough to invite his friends over for a meal for which they do the cooking. He is quick to add that he feels very supported by family, friends and the Brotherhood, which keeps him sane.

Tom has booked himself into a course about acquired brain injury, partly to understand his own condition but also because it may give him insight into the needs of others. He declares that

Adam is a 'hero', and says everyone agrees: Adam stretches people's capabilities, working one-to-one on their personal goals. Importantly, Adam is teaching Tom to work with other people who have similar problems, which has helped him realise that not everything has to centre on him, that others have needs too. Tom has learnt, through Adam, 'to do the best you can'. There is new life and he is grateful for the meaningful friendships he has found with the people that care for him.

Elizabeth **Alfred**

Elizabeth was born on 10 January 1914; it is difficult to offer a snapshot of a woman who, at the age of 94, is still acutely active. When she was 79, Elizabeth was ordained as a priest in the Anglican Church in the diocese of Melbourne. She was way beyond retirement age, but this was seen as a recognition of her tremendous life's work as missioner, teacher and pastoral support to many clergy and people of the churches, schools and agencies with which she has served. It was a thank-you, as it were, but Elizabeth saw it too as an indication that she still had significant ministry left in her.

Elizabeth was a country girl and lived in Victorian regional centres like Yarrawonga and Bendigo, but she was equally at home in suburbs like Fitzroy and Dandenong; in her great old age, she offered generous and gracious ministry to the people of Carrum Downs and the Tucker Settlement. She remembers a night in the 1940s when she attended a fellowship evening at St John's Church in La Trobe Street in Melbourne. Here she was challenged by a comment made by a member of the fellowship, Mrs Baker, who said, 'A worthwhile Christian should be doing a worthwhile job in the world'. It was on this night that Elizabeth met Father Tucker, who was speaking of his vision of establishing a low-cost residential settlement at Carrum Downs, for the many people who were living in extreme poverty in places like Fitzroy. He made the comments, 'If I get the man, I'll get the money' and 'If the thing is right, we'll get it right'.

'Tucker was charismatic,' says Elizabeth. 'People responded to his call to ministry and action, and were wholeheartedly drawn into his vision for the elimination of poverty.

'I was deeply impressed by his vision. He could see the potential of 34 acres of bushland for such a settlement: first of all for young families from Fitzroy; and then, after the war, for elderly people.' As the settlement progressed and grew, Elizabeth got on with her own ministry, becoming connected both to Father Tucker through the parish of St James in Dandenong and to Father Michael Clark, a long-time friend of Tucker and a member of the Order of the Brotherhood of St Laurence. Elizabeth commented then that she wanted to live at Carrum Downs when she retired. 'Father Tucker laughed at me because it was such a long way off, but I never changed my mind and at the end of October in 1978 I came to live here.'

Elizabeth was resigned to the thought that her ministry would never be priestly. Ordained a deaconess in 1944, she knew that making her way in the world and the Church was never going to be easy, that she would mostly be seen in terms of a support worker in its male-dominated culture. But in fact her ministry journey offered her opportunities for personal, spiritual and experiential growth, which made her an invaluable member of the Church. There are few Anglican agencies and bodies, particularly in the diocese of Melbourne, that Elizabeth hasn't touched with her wisdom and counsel, and it would be true to say that it hasn't all been niceties – she has had to be pretty tough on some of her stands in keeping the Church on the straight and narrow.

The night before Elizabeth's ordination in 1991, then-journalist Mary Delahunty asked the question, 'Don't you think, Reverend Alfred, that opening the doors to women in the priesthood will attract a lot of strange women?' Elizabeth raised an eyebrow, smiled, offered her characteristic chuckle and responded, 'There are an awful lot of strange men in the priesthood.' Many of us who have the honour of working with her and stood together that night (all men) laughed and raised a glass to her.

'Suddenly the ascended Jesus became present to me. For me it was the great step forward in my spiritual life.'

Elizabeth's spiritual life helps us to understand the whole of her life's journey. When she was fifteen she heard someone ask the question, 'Do you ever take Jesus with you on your daily walk?' In that moment, Jesus was brought to life for her: 'Suddenly the ascended Jesus became present to me. For me it was the great step forward in my spiritual life.' Attending church, singing hymns and reflecting on scripture are the things that add flesh to her spiritual bones; through the bread and wine she receives during the Eucharist she receives life and courage from her Jesus, who feeds and sustains the poor and those who seek justice.

Elizabeth has never been frightened of the good journey and even in her 70s and 80s she would lead groups of people to the Holy Land to explore and discover both the bigger world and their Christian roots. There is a marvellous photo, taken by one of her companions, of Elizabeth marching forth in sensible shoes and tweeds and what looks like a gardening hat, wielding a walking stick above her head and giving physical expression to the commands 'Go forth' and 'Follow me'.

But while she's proud of her energetic life and her travels and various ministries, Elizabeth is still on the journey and isn't ready yet to relinquish her participation in the stuff of life. There have been occasions when she has been surrounded by hundreds of people who have come together to celebrate the benefits they have received through her vocational life, and at times those moments have been truly emotional and appropriate recognition of her gifts.

Sitting with her in her well-ordered room at Carrum Downs, you are surrounded by images, photos and memorabilia of a life that has spanned the best part of a century. Photos of her beloved parents, handsome and strong; a painting which she has hung above her bed wherever she has been throughout her life; paintings she has made of places in which she has lived and travelled; photos of the Holy Land and of the Queen, whom she loves and admires. And beside her bed a prayer book, a bible, a *Woman's Day* and a good novel – the things that at once sustain her spiritual life, keep her in the real world and allow her to 'travel' to other places.

Elizabeth is still on the journey and isn't ready yet to relinquish her participation in the stuff of life.

Elizabeth is a good person and a good priest, and the ministry she continues to offer day-to-day to other members of the Carrum Downs Settlement reminds us all of the importance of community and friendship, as well as being an expression of her love of Jesus. It's not certain what Father Tucker found in Elizabeth, but it would be true to say that his vision, keen sense of social justice and discomfort with the status quo were embraced by Elizabeth too. As a result, her connection with him while she was at Dandenong made her an excellent ambassador for his grassroots philosophy in relation to the Carrum Downs Settlement. His innovation gave her the opportunity to serve God, and the people the Brotherhood cares for, through her continued ministry in what is also rightfully her home. 'Let your light so shine before all people that they may see your good works and glorify your Father who is in heaven.' Amen!

Hazel **Ball**

'The more we are together, the happier we will be. For your friends are my friends, and my friends are your friends. The more we are together the happier we will be . . .' When a song needs to be sung, Hazel will sing this one and it encapsulates all that she believes in. The first time I met Hazel she was in full flight, playing the piano at the Coolibah Centre and encouraging me to join in the weekly singalong. There was a group of people around the table, Coolibah members, and some of them the most unlikely singers, but Hazel had in one way or another convinced them, persuaded them, to be part of the group.

Singing, for Hazel, is an expression of all that lies in the soul, and she has believed for much of her life that 'If only we could get everyone to sing!' what a different world it would be. It is interesting to note that, of all the activities offered at Coolibah over the many years Hazel has offered this ministry, her group was the best and most consistently attended. And right up to the day she suffered a minor stroke, aged 95, she was still commanding the same attention and enthusiasm. She had song books printed and never

begrudged a request for an unfamiliar song, which she would seek out, learn and add to the repertoire for the next session.

This diminutive lady, sitting on a cushion on the piano stool, would throw herself at the keyboard, arms flying up and down, with all the confidence and passion of great players like Winifred Atwell. And while she'd play she would constantly turn her head to make sure her audience were doing what they were there for – to sing and have some joy in their lives. God help you if you interrupted the schedule; that time belonged to her and her little band of friends each week, and that was that! Community life is all that matters to Hazel: togetherness brings compassion and love, and therefore is the ideal of the living Christ. This is important in understanding her integrity, and her journey.

Hazel's journey has been a long one, from her birthplace in Colombo, Sri Lanka (then Ceylon), in 1910 through three marriages to her finally settling in Melbourne. Her parents Clarebell and Julian Anderiesz were Burghers, members of a Ceylonese/Dutch ethnic group. Her father worked with the railways and she remembers having a lovely childhood and an 'upper-class life'. All the generations of her family lived under the same roof, in her grandfather's house; he was a rich man who worked with the Ceylonese national bank and it seems they enjoyed a secure life where there was much happiness. Hazel attended the convent school run by Irish nuns a short walk from home. Her many school friends were mostly from well-to-do families, the daughters of professionals and academics. She learned all the skills that a young lady in her circumstances should learn, like sewing and knitting and music. Playing the piano has been one of the great joys that has sustained her throughout her life. She speaks highly of the Irish nuns: 'They were good people, patient and loving.' She remembers loving sports, particularly netball, basketball and tennis, and she was the school captain of all these activities. There was another captain who was a Tamil girl, Penathwaghy, and they had a deal that whoever won the other would cheer for.

In Hazel's childhood, Colombo was a destination for international trade. As the world was opening up there was money to be made in the development of its infrastructure, albeit usually at the expense of the nationals, who were paid little for their labours. Local poverty and the culture of begging on the streets became an ever-present ugliness in the cities, even as foreigners were moving in to take advantage of the opportunities available. A Frenchman by the name of Montague ('Monty') Dels Harp, a motor engineer, came seeking work in Colombo and gained employment with one of the companies. On seeing Hazel, then in her mid-teens, he commented to a companion, 'I'm going to marry that girl'. Hazel refers to him as 'the best man in my life, the father of my children!'

Theirs was, she remembers, a big wedding in the Catholic church, and she was eighteen or nineteen. After their marriage they moved to Hatton, a tea-plantation centre located more than 1500 metres above sea level. It was a happy home, and their three children were born there: Neilia, who died of cancer when only young; Neal; and Villette. But soon after the last child was born, Monty, who had been born with a heart condition, died of heart failure and Hazel was left a widow.

Later Hazel met a widower called Forbes; they married in Ceylon, but he died too – Hazel remembers very little about this man. Soon after his death, Hazel migrated to Australia with her adult daughter and they settled in Melbourne, where they had friends in Clifton Hill. She became connected to the local church and was soon playing the organ there. She married Father Leo Ball, an Anglican priest and a widower, and cared for him until his death.

Hazel came to the Coolibah as a volunteer, playing the piano and establishing her legendary singalong group. Because of the stroke and her age she plays less and less these days and she has moved to Sumner House, our aged-care facility in Fitzroy. Given the length of her service to the Coolibah, many of the long-term members know and respect her deeply. It is interesting to note that we have lately brought two communion services together because the group not attending the same service as Hazel's were constantly asking about her welfare. Their coming together has brought a greater sense of peace to the gathering, and a sense of relief that

Hazel is still present and being looked after – one of the great benefits for the community that lives and gathers on the Brunswick Street site.

Hazel has unswerving faith and an old-fashioned sense of propriety laced with old-fashioned Victorian pride. She has become a frail little old woman who is concerned about the world she has been left in, but knows Jesus still walks with her. She is impatient and doesn't like her focus to be interrupted: as she is wheeled into the sitting-room at Sumner House for the weekly communion service, she will openly express her annoyance at what she sees to be distracting and sometimes banal conversation that has nothing to do with what she has come to be part of. 'Have we come here to talk about the football or are we here to worship God!' An immediate silence falls over the dozen or so people who have gathered, though there is at least one who will come straight back at her and tell her to stop whingeing. Hazel will laugh, somewhat embarrassed.

In her old age and in her longing to meet God face to face, Hazel sees little point in conversations that don't point her in the direction she desires to go in. There is always a kiss for her priest and her own offering of a blessing to the attending priest; she will share a joke with the priest, which she wouldn't with others, which is maybe a mark of her privileged background or maybe the privilege of the widow of a priest. She listens intently to every word you speak, for every word to her is part of her ongoing prayer. After

Mass has ended, if she's feeling up to it someone will help her to the piano and she will begin to play a medley of the tunes she remembers – they are slower and more deliberate these days, and at times a little confused, and more and more she'll hold her hands up and politely decline to play because there is too much pain in her fingers. However, Hazel reflects at the end of the day, 'I can live without a husband, but I can't live without my piano'.

'The more we are together, the happier we will be. For your friends are my friends, and my friends are your friends. The more we are together the happier we will be . . .'

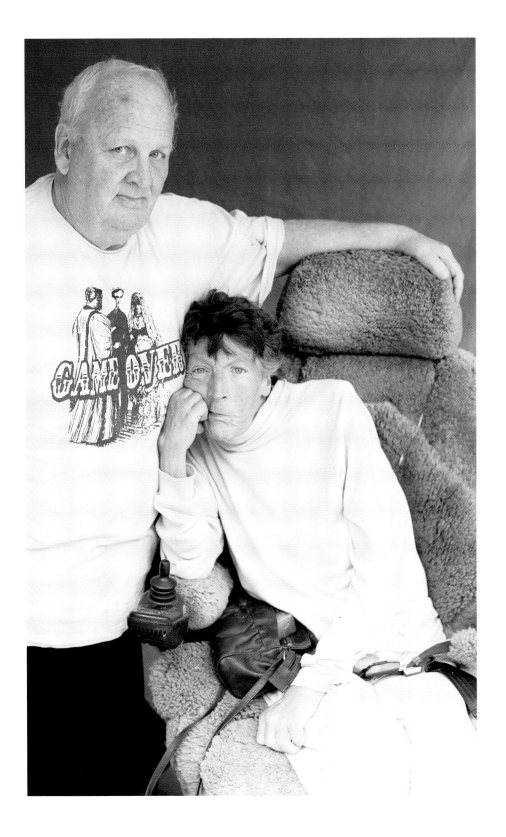

Rod **and Rhonda**

There was a big 1960s ambulance parked out the front, with menacing tinted windows and official signs, but the indicators that it was an emergency vehicle had been painted over. Many of those vehicles look sinister in their later years, no matter how clean and neat, and this one was no exception. But it is the pride and joy of Rod, who found it wasting away, destined for the tip, and knew straight away that it was just what he needed! He took it home, made it work again, and fitted it out with a hydraulic lift at the back so that he could raise without effort his beloved partner Rhonda.

The vehicle is, as Rod says, 'a private version of the specialist taxis you see around the place, but it's our very own!'

Rod is a big man of 54 who spent most of his working life down a mine. He met Rhonda at Hampton Park Rehabilitation Centre, which he was attending because of chronic back pain. Rhonda, a pretty, petite woman, suffered a stroke in 1997 as a result of high blood pressure and stress; she had managed a busy restaurant and reception centre in St Kilda Road. Rod was a keen greyhound trainer; he collapsed one day when his 'back caved in' while he was walking his dogs. Both ended up in Hampton Park Rehab, where they developed an enduring friendship.

Rhonda's stroke left her severely paralysed down one side and impaired her walking. As often happens after such trauma, her marriage failed; hampered in her ability to care for herself, and having no apparent close family to support her, she ended up in a hostel.

When Rhonda and Rod met, Rod had been happily married for 33 years but his wife had tragically died of cancer. Rod needed companionship, and the friendship that began to flourish between them became a special bond. As Rod visited Rhonda in the hostel, he began to be concerned about what he saw as her decline in health, both physically and emotionally. He was uncomfortable about the way staff treated her as though she had only a short time to live. 'I was shocked when I saw how she declined month by month, and the way she was being treated. It wasn't the Rhonda that I had seen at the rehab centre. I knew she would be better off living with me, but this thought was met with strong opposition from both the hostel and Rhonda's family.'

Rod's capacity to care for Rhonda was questioned. 'People would tell me that she would be dead in no time flat, and ask me how I was going to help shower her and organise her meals. But I had no choice, as she was going downhill fast – and I was prepared to take the risk, rather than see her so unhappy and neglected.' The dispute culminated in a 'guardianship hearing' that paved the way for Rhonda to come and live with Rod. He had to meet the challenge that he set for himself, and to quell the family's lack of confidence in him, and their suspicions. This was all exacerbated by the reality that their first months together were sheer hard work, and exhausting. His home was not well suited to such specialised care, and they both struggled with chronic illness and disability.

Rod and Rhonda will both tell you that social workers do not rate highly on their Most Trusted list. (Their definition of a social worker is 'Any health professional who has any control or influence over our life!') At one stage they handed the management of their affairs to the State Trustees; it was a difficult and painful time, and deciding to regain control meant twelve months of agony and frustration, which ended up in VCAT, having to prove that they could manage budgets. The great frustration, as Rod saw it, was that all the hard work they had put into establishing what has become a loving relationship was put to the test by the suspicious, 'We know better than you about these things' attitude of those they both saw as interfering bureaucrats. They remained determined that Rhonda would not re-enter residential care, and that they would nurture what they perceived to be a deepening and loving relationship.

Rod becomes emotional when recounting all that he and

Rhonda have achieved. They have been able to demonstrate responsible management of their financial, medical and living needs with properly programmed help, a good routine, and Rod's incredible ability to network in the community close to where they live. Rod took Rhonda into all the shops they knew they would need to frequent: they introduced themselves and carefully explained their needs, particularly Rhonda's. They then set about supporting their local community, who have in turn welcomed them with open arms. Sensible living. The locals know when they are around, of course, because of the 'Rod and Rhonda mobile' parked out front! It has a sticker on the back asking for people's courtesy in not parking too close, so that Rhonda can get in and out as easily as possible.

> For them independence remains important, so they have been careful in their choice of carers when possible, and in choosing places and networks where they feel safe and happy.

For them independence remains important, so they have been careful in their choice of carers when possible, and in choosing places and networks where they feel safe and happy. Rhonda had a Care Package with the Brotherhood, and while Rod was suspicious of the social worker at first, he found a true ally in

Mrs Dodd. She helped them to manage, would call in any time, and built a strong, trusting and reliable relationship with them which considerably helped them build a sense of independence, particularly with home and personal care.

Strangely enough, part of the connection Rod and Rhonda enjoy is their fierce independence. They also share a love of exercise, which they see as a way of remaining fit and out of the clutches of the health and aged-care system. Being older than Rhonda, Rod wants to keep in shape so he can provide the best level of care for her: 'I work out for at least an hour a day and often more if I am feeling motivated. Being active is the best way I can guarantee that I will be able to manage Rhonda's daily care needs.' He recognises that Rhonda's electric wheelchair was a mixed blessing, giving her greater independence but unfortunately making her less active. No longer having to use her leg and arm muscles to manoeuvre a wheelchair, Rhonda's strength and flexibility declined. 'I was sitting in the chair all day and I felt myself getting weaker and weaker.'

Rhonda found out through her care manager about the physical activities provided by the Brotherhood's socialisation program. 'I was really interested in the water aerobics and Adam's fitness classes, but at first I was nervous about joining. What pushed me was the desire not to sit at home and vegetate – I wanted to get out and meet people.' Rod's involvement made it easier for Rhonda to participate in Adam's classes, as there was someone to encourage her. 'Exercise isn't easy for me, as I am always in pain due to my arthritis. I don't like exercise. I used to walk short distances unaided, but now I need help. Walking makes me feel good and motivated – that's why I like the water aerobics, as it takes away the fear of falling.'

They are usually first to arrive at the fitness class, parking the 'ambo' out the front. They sit at the front door waiting for everyone to arrive, and there is much greeting and kindness as people gather. This is a safe and supportive place, and Rod and Rhonda have developed warm friendships; they all look out for one another. There is a seriousness about what they have come for, but at the same time there is fun about their awkwardness and limitations as a dedicated Adam takes them through their paces one by one.

Rod is never dull: he is a ladies' man, but he is also an activist and if he sees an injustice he'll speak out. He has no fear! Life has been too tough for him to take things lying down – builder's labourer, plasterer, union rep, greyhound trainer and more; he has seen a lot and he has had a lot to say. But he has a heart of gold and his love for Rhonda is an outward sign of something deep and unmistakeably kind. His ability to see past his own immense pain to the need of another, to show kindness and love, speaks highly of the man. Rhonda is resolved, grateful and a little philosophical too: he is worth taking the extra effort for – in his own way, he has given her life.

About the
Brotherhood of
St Laurence

Established during the Great Depression of the 1930s, the Brotherhood of St Laurence was the creation of Father Gerard Tucker. It has
developed into an independent national organisation that provides
services and programs to disadvantaged parents and children, the
long-term unemployed, vulnerable older people, and refugees.

As well as on-the-ground services, the Brotherhood under-
takes research into the causes of poverty and develops policies
to improve the situation of those people that it seeks to help. The
Brotherhood focuses on the four transition stages considered critical to future wellbeing:

- the early years, both at home and in school
- the years from school to work and further education
- the periods in and out of work, whether voluntary or
  involuntary
- retirement and ageing

There are numerous ways that you can help the Brotherhood achieve its vision of an Australia free of poverty. By contributing your time, skills or ideas, or by donating money or goods, you can make a real difference to disadvantaged Australians.

Working for an Australia free of poverty

Brotherhood of St Laurence
Working for an Australia free of poverty

67 Brunswick Street
Fitzroy VIC 3065

Phone (03) 9483 1301
Fax (03) 9483 1336
Email donate@bsl.org.au
www.bsl.org.au

All donations to the Brotherhood of St Laurence of $2 and over are tax deductible

Please find enclosed my gift of:
☐$25   ☐$50   ☐$100   ☐$200   ☐$_____my choice

I wish to join the Brotherhood's regular giving program and give a tax-deductible monthly donation.

☐Please deduct monthly donations of $_____from the credit card below, until further notice.

☐Please deduct monthly donations of $_____from my bank account by Direct Debit, until further notice. (The Brotherhood will forward a Direct Debit authority for you to sign.)

Payment method: ☐Cheque   ☐Money Order   ☐Visa   ☐MasterCard
☐DinersClub   ☐AMEX Amex ID _ _ _ _

Card Number _ _ _ _ /_ _ _ _ /_ _ _ _ /_ _ _ _ Expiration Date _ _ /_ _
Name on Card_____ Signature_____
Street Address_____
Suburb_____ Postcode_____
Telephone (H)_____ (W)_____

☐Please send me information about including the Brotherhood of St Laurence in my Will.
* BSL BLD

We respect the privacy of your personal details. The Brotherhood of St Laurence will not disclose your details to any other party. See our Privacy Policy on our website.